Heartcry for China

Ross Paterson

with
Rod Boreham

D1125769

Sovereign World

© 1989 Ross Paterson

Sovereign World Ltd.
P.O. Box 17
Chichester PO20 6YB

All rights reserved. No part of this publication may be reproduced, stored in a retrieval system, or transmitted, in any form, or by any means, mechanical, electronic, photocopying or otherwise, without the prior written consent of the publisher.

Short extracts may be used for review purposes.

All biblical quotations are from The Holy Bible: New International Version, Copyright © 1973, 1978, 1984 International Bible Society.
Published in the U.K. by Hodder & Stoughton and in the U.S.A., by Zondervan Bible Publishers.

ISBN 1 85240 036 6

Printed and bound in Great Britain by
Richard Clay Ltd., Bungay, Suffolk

CONTENTS

To Christine
My "Airen".

and
Deborah, Hannah, Sharon, Joanna and Esther
My "five gold flowers".

FOREWORD

"For Christ's love compels us, because we are convinced that one died for all, and therefore all died. And he died for all, that those who live should no longer live for themselves but for him who died for them and was raised again . . ."
2 Corinthians 5:14,15 NIV

Ross Paterson has written a compelling book about a compelling love. It speaks in simple and moving terms about Christ's love for the great nation of China; it speaks of the extraordinary new life evidenced there through his death; it speaks of what may yet come about there through his life.

I knew Ross by reputation some years before I was privileged to know him as a friend and recognised in him the qualities of a man of God. He had made brave choices which were against the tide of the times and it was clear that these came from an intimate relationship with Jesus and obedience to his voice. Even this book is a result of the choices he speaks of in the last chapter. I believe that through the information and passion contained within, many will hear the voice that begged him to be its mouthpiece.

I would advise it as required reading for those concerned in any way with the Far East. I would also recommend it to all who claim to be followers of Jesus Christ — with the prayer — that it be used as a tool in the universal commission.

Jackie Pullinger *Hong Kong.*
July 1989

"We have waited eagerly for this book. This is no remote account but the inside story of the church in China. Step into the powerful dimension of Chinese spirituality from one who breathes it. You will never want to leave it. This is more than an account of ways to help the church in China".

John Wallis *(UK Director, Overseas Missionary Fellowship).*

"I highly recommend Ross Paterson and his ministry to China and to the oriental community worldwide. Ross has one of the most prepared and effective ministries to this significant world culture. I know of no-one who has more clear and emphatic insights into their needs for Christ".

Charles Simpson *(Chairman of CSM and Fellowship of Covenant Ministers and Churches U.S.A.).*

"CHINA! The world's largest nation – a battleground of contending ideologies, a scene of countless miracles and martyrdoms, a harvest field ready to be reaped. No-one is better qualified than Ross Paterson to depict the crises and the challenge of China today.

He served for ten years as a missionary in Taiwan where he taught in a university. He is fluent in Mandarin Chinese and intimately acquainted with the current situation in Mainland China.

Ross is a man with a vision, but not a visionary. With a heart full of love and a mind that is analytical and penetrating, he challenges every sincere Christian in the free world to sacrifice commitment on behalf of our fellow believers in China. God has given the Western Church an opportunity to be His instruments in one of the greatest moves of the Holy Spirit in all church history. May we not be found wanting!"

Derek Prince *(Author and International Bible Teacher)*

"The eyes of the world are on China today. But who can tell us what God is doing there? Few are more qualified than Ross Paterson, but Ross has no appetite for mere morsels of information. His purpose is undisguised. He wants you stirred and involved. He cares passionately for China's millions, and wants you to care too. As you read this book, open your heart and mind and ask God what your response should be to this one-fifth of the world's population".

Terry Virgo (Leader, New Frontiers International)

INTRODUCTION

This book sets out to report the real needs of the Chinese churches and to challenge Christians worldwide to face up to those needs. We need to reach out to our Chinese brethren. It was birthed and partly written before June 1989, but to give some perspective on recent events, an additional chapter has been inserted. However, the heartcry of this book was formed long before the tanks rolled in to Tiananmen Square. I have been in close touch with developments in the Chinese church for some time now. I have made trips to China and have met with church leaders and fellowshipped with congregations. They want the world to know the truth about their situation. Although their real names are written in heaven, I have made some changes to protect their identities. This book is written for your urgent attention on their behalf.

It is unlikely that the images of Tiananmen Square will be quickly forgotten by even the most hardened foreign observers. They are burned on to our memories. China has, however, other images and another heartcry — that of its growing Christian church. That church has suffered too — perhaps, collectively over the years, it has suffered more than the students we have seen on our television sets. My plea is that Christians must not forget the needs of those Chinese people. We must be sensitive to their heartcry.

In co-operation with others, I have personally been making a practical response to their needs for teaching materials and radio broadcasts. We have achieved much within a short space of time but the materials we have sent in are but a drop in an ocean of need. The harvest field is vast – more than one fifth of the world's population live in China – but the labourers are few.

This book is a practical one. It contains suggestions for believers who want to help influence China's future. It is not a scholarly work. I do not know if I am capable of that. My heart keeps getting in the way. I trust that you will bear with me. I want this book to help many servants of Christ to consider what they can do for China.

There are many who have helped with it. Rod Boreham did much early research and writing for it and Tom Ross helped with the finishing touches. Chris Mungeam told me to write it and has been so much help along the way. I owe much to Chris and to Jan. My staff in York raced gainst deadlines for me – Peter Conde, Valerie Dean, Judith Corbishley and Wendy Neary, along with Sue Wooff. I want to thank them for that and for so much more. A host of China colleagues have given so much over the years – especially Tony Lambert and Lesley Francis. There are many others – most of them appear in the book. Acomb Christian Fellowship have prayed with me and been patient with me. The Lord has given me marvellous comrades in that church. Alex & Peggy Buchanan and Harry & Betty Hughes know how much I owe to them. My parents and Christine's have given so much to us and we thank them.

The book is dedicated to Christine and the girls. They are precious gifts from the Lord and I thank Him for them. They know more than any around me the cost of China.

Finally, there are my brothers and sisters in China. Thank you for walking with the Lord Jesus; thank you for living – and dying – for Him.

"My soul yearns, oh how intensely, for the evangelisation of the 180 millions (*now 1000 millions*) of these unoccupied provinces. Oh, that I had a hundred lives to give or spend for their good!"

"One third of the human family is in China, needing the Gospel. 12 millions (*now many more*) there are passing beyond the reach of that Gospel every year. If you want hard work and little appreciation; if you value God's approval more than you fear men's disapprobation; if you are prepared to take joyfully the spoiling of your goods, and seal your testimony, if need be, with your blood; if you can pity and love Chinese, you may count on a harvest of souls now and a crown of glory hereafter 'that fadeth not away', and on the Master's 'Well done'."

Hudson Taylor's "An appeal for prayer on behalf of more than 150 millions of Chinese." Dated 1875. (Italics mine).

CHAPTER 1

THE BIRTH OF THIS BOOK

I do not want to begin at the beginning. I want to begin by sharing with you a conversation I had with a couple involved in church leadership in China, because what they said to me represents, in one sense, the birthplace of this book. Of course there have been many other times and places and voices over the years — both before and after theirs. But from them came a special word to me — a heartcry from China. And so there is no better place to begin than there.

"Please be a reporter for us", they said, *"We have no means by which our voice can be heard by others, inside or outside of China. Simply say to our brothers and sisters outside of China: 'Some people tell one story, and their voice is heard. But others are telling a different story, and their voice is not being heard'."*

It was the early 1980's in Shanghai, the most populous of China's many large cities. There are about 12 million people in that one city alone, with another 37 or so cities in China each with over one million people. China at that time was going through one of its frequent changes — or lurches — politically and socially. Indeed at that

1

very time, the Gang of Four, who had so brutalised the nation during the period of the Cultural Revolution in China, were on trial for their crimes against the nation and the people of China. A different leadership was in charge, with new and much more open policies, at least in the economic sphere. The curtain that separated China from the rest of the world had been somewhat pulled aside, so that we could see a little of them and they of us. The Chinese were beginning to breathe again — though very carefully, for there had been so much suffering and death during that dark period from 1966 to 1976, and the pain and suspicion were still very real.

I considered the couple before me in that simple room. I knew that Mr and Mrs Chen, Renguang and Enhui, were Christian leaders, undertaking to help lead and feed spiritually many believers in and around the city. I knew that they were of an age to have walked through the early days of Marxism in China in the 1950's, followed by the yet more difficult days of the Cultural Revolution in China in the late 60's and early 70's. That meant that what they said did not come out of an immature or hot-headed enthusiasm; their words were born out of many years of suffering for the Lord Jesus Christ and for His gospel. I knew also that they loved the Lord Jesus deeply — that their zeal for Him was as real as ever.

I had been nervous and excited as I approached the address that I had been given, for it was one of the first visits of that kind that I had made in China. It was in fact my first visit to the Mainland, though I already had quite broad experience in China ministries, and had previously lived in Taiwan for ten years. But this was China, and it was different. But as I had sat with them, and been welcomed by them because of the mutual friend whose name I had mentioned, it was clear that, whatever they might have walked through in the last few decades, their love for the Lord Jesus burned bright. I was at ease with them.

2

I was astonished and even amused at the response they made to the Christian literature and tapes that I had handed over to them. If only my Christian friends outside China could see what I was seeing! Here were these two saints, well on in years, behaving like my children do when they are given their birthday presents — Renguang and Enhui were excited and thrilled as they took out the books and tapes that would mean spiritual food for them to share with others.

I was struck by the way in which they came straight to the point. Oriental folk often tend to be polite and diffident before coming to the main point of what they say. But the Chens clearly trusted me and wanted no delays. I think that they must have sat down before I arrived and prepared a "shopping list" of topics on which they needed material. And now I scribbled hasty notes in my little notebook, grateful that they spoke clear Mandarin Chinese without a local Shanghai dialect. They urgently needed teaching materials on a number of topics — concerning the Christian walk after salvation, prophetic fulfilment of the word of God, the work of the Holy Spirit, the Christian and the State, plus various other matters. How wonderful it would be if many believers from abroad could see what I was seeing — the hunger for the word of God, the way in which books and tapes were snapped up, and more asked for, almost before they were out of the bag in which they had been brought.

I have no doubt that this kind of sight, in my early China impressions, made a deep impact on me. I have lived in two worlds since then — based in York in the North of England, yet working, travelling and speaking often in the realm of China's church. Our world is so well served by Bible teaching ministries, conferences, colleges, book and tapes. The other world, China, is hungry for those ministries that it so seriously lacks. That inequality impresses and burdens all who touch men and women like the Chens in China today.

3

And now they were making a request of me — that I should help them in a specific way. *"Be a reporter for us"*, they were saying. I knew what they meant, from experience already gained in my work as China Coordinator in the United Kingdom for the Overseas Missionary Fellowship (formerly the China Inland Mission under Hudson Taylor). The Chens felt that the churches in China were not being honestly represented by the voices that claimed to speak for all of China's church, voices that often differed in theology from them and multitudes of others both in spiritual passion and in practical requests for help. The Chens could not agree with the statements made by these other voices that China's fast growing churches did not need radio broadcasts or Bibles and spiritual books and tapes. They knew that many Christians in China were hungry for any help that they could get, indeed prepared to take great risks to get that help, because of the danger of their going wrong in their spiritual walk for the lack of Bibles and Biblical teaching. Many were coming to the Lord in China in the late seventies and the early eighties, as the nation began to open up, and the Chens knew that it would not do to ignore their cries for spiritual help.

"Be a reporter for us", the Chens had said. They wanted me simply to show Christians outside of China what the needs of the many, many believers in China's numerous churches are, as we work together with others who try to do the same thing. The Chens and many like them do not have a voice to tell you, whoever you may be that read this book, what their needs are. You have not gone or cannot go to them, and the vast majority of them cannot come to you. And so they need "reporters" in the middle to try, as best we can, to share faithfully what they are saying. We make mistakes, we misunderstand and misinterpret. But we do at least try to serve them.

Some may say that we are wrong to act as such reporters. They say that we should only attend to the voice of the 'official' church leaders in China. Do they,

4

these 'official' leaders, not speak for China's church? This is the heart of the problem which the Chens were addressing when they said: *'Some people tell one story, and their voice is heard. But others are telling a different story, and their voice is not being heard.'* They are burdened by the fact that they do not have a voice, and cannot say what they feel, nor share what they need. Should we say that we will listen to the 'some people' and their opinions, without giving any attention to 'others'? If so, we fail to acknowledge the rights of that 'other' leadership that has also been appointed by God, and has paid a high price for their faithfulness. Are we to reward that by screening them out of our spiritual consciousness?

Others argue that nobody can know what is going on in China, nobody can understand the situation well enough to form a judgment that really represents in any significant way the church in China. Any view other than the official one will be based on the views of only a small number of people, and will be insufficient at best and deceptive at worst. It is a fact that China experts have a saying that you can find proof to substantiate almost any statement you may choose to make about China. The nation is so big and its people so many that somewhere and sometime you can find evidence of anything you choose to say! The picture is so diverse in China, this argument runs, and the churches are so many and disparate, that there is no such thing as a unheard church voice that can claim to speak for more than just a few Christians.

I do not agree. There certainly is much diversity in China's church. Equally, there are certainly no evangelical church leaders' annual conferences in China, from which carefully worded documents of accord may emerge! But the constant interchange of reports and instructions, from sources both inside and outside of China, helps us to establish a composite picture. The evidence that the Chens placed before me that night is manifestly there — for those who want to see it. I knew that I was talking that night in Shanghai to leaders of a group of churches in the largest city in China. Their views were not those of an irrelevant minority, but of a networking of like minds amongst Christians in different parts of China, not just in Shanghai. Indeed, as the years have passed, the general picture that they shared that night has become clearer and clearer, evidenced over and over again by reported and personal contacts from many parts of China.

The Chens asked me to be *a* reporter, not *the* reporter. That is all I seek to do, relaying to you one voice from China's church.

When all is said and done (and I think sometimes that there is more said than done about China amongst most believers), the basic facts are both simple and clear:

Firstly, the church in China is growing, and in some areas it is growing with revival intensity. Some have said that it is the fastest growing church in the world.

Secondly, that growth has brought tremendous needs for pastoring and teaching, as folk with scarcely any idea about the kingdom of the Lord Jesus Christ have been swept into faith in Him. A doctor in Northern China told me the story of a recent convert, a sister, who had got into a fierce verbal battle with another person. Words had been exchanged, and no doubt some pretty violent statements were made. When this young believer in Jesus came to herself and repented before the Lord Jesus, she was so upset, and so keen to show her genuine repentance, that she took decisive action — she cut off her tongue. Why? Because someone, somewhere had said that you should cut off the member of your body that offends rather than to enter into hell with it. We may be horrified at that, but we can also be humbled by her zeal for the Lord. That is typical of China. A zeal to obey the Lord with sometimes little idea of what the Bible says, of how a Christian should walk and behave. What else can we expect if we understand that there are

6

still churches of a thousand people with only a few Bibles and hardly any Christian teaching books among them? Pastors weep in China when they go to seek for Bibles and books and are told there are none. They know that the needs are so great and the stakes are so high.

Thirdly, many Christians welcome help from their brothers and sisters in countries outside of China. Of course there are conditions to that help. It must be under the leadership and direction of the pastors in China, and it must be to serve them, not to carve out some name or empire for ourselves. But they do long for us to pray for and serve them, to share our bread with them, so that they may feed their flocks, and thus obey the command of the Lord Jesus.

That is also why the Chens and many others are frustrated by their lack of a voice. But more than that, they are frustrated by the failure of many believers outside China to understand the need for 'reporters' who will give a wider picture of China's church scene. Do we not understand, they might ask, that Marxist governments work by controlling the information that comes out of their country on any subject? Surely after we have seen the two totally different versions of the events in the Tiananmen Square in June 1989 (the Chinese government's and that of the world's reporters), we can understand that truth is a highly negotiable commodity in China's State-run media context. Do we not see that that is true of believers in China too — and hear them when they say that they would like voices that we can hear, for they do not have any under that system?

Yes, we run risks if we claim in any way to "report" for them — risks that we misrepresent or paint a false picture in some way. But if we walk with the Lord and are careful, surely some kind of effort to do something, with all the attendant risks, is better than a failure to hear the cry for help coming from the hearts of our Chinese fellow believers? We must recognise that they also are God's appointed leaders under Jesus, the Head of the

Church — that is exactly why we need to hear their voice — and to respond!

★★★★★★★★★★★★★★★★

Renguang insisted on seeing me to the bus stop that night as I left his house. I did not want him to, for it seemed to me unnecessary that we should be out at night on the streets of Shanghai together. He did not see it that way. The Chinese are a deeply courteous people, and take seriously the need to "song" — to see you on your way. You are required to say "bu-song, bu-song" ("don't send me on my way") to your host, as he stands outside the place where he lives or walks away from that place along the road with you as you depart. When he judges he has gone far enough, he will bid you farewell and return to his house, as you go on your way. Renguang was clearly determined to go on with me right to the bus stop, in spite of my protestation. Perhaps it was the only way at his disposal to thank me and those like me for caring for the church in China.

As we stood at the bus stop, suddenly, without any warning, a man in the queue turned and barked a question at him. Looking at me, he snapped at Renguang: "What does he have to do with you?". Here was the other China, where men and women — even children — watch each other to report to the security police, and thus gain favour for themselves. It is the China of the accusation, of the betrayal, of the willingness to bring massive harm to another for state or personal ends.

Renguang was not caught out — he had obviously been in that kind of a situation before. Responding to the man about me, he simply said: "He is a friend of my Father". To the man, in the early eighties, a time when foreigners were becoming more and more frequent in China and the Chinese had begun to travel abroad again, that seemed satisfactory. Obviously he assumed that I

8

had met Renguang's father in the West, or that I had met him professionally in another city. But I knew what Renguang really meant — that in Christ Jesus there is no East or West, China or America or Africa or Australia or France or Britain. There are only those who know and love Jesus, those who have received Him as Saviour and Lord — and also, on the other hand, those who have not. That is the only distinction — do we know and love the Lord Jesus Christ? Race, nationality, colour and background mean nothing in those divine and ultimate terms. Renguang was acknowledging a relationship that will last for eternity, as we go to be together with Jesus and dwell for ever with our common Father — our heavenly Father God. The blood of Jesus has cleansed from sin and the new life of God is within us already — whether we be Chinese or not.

At any rate, the questioner seemed satisfied, and the incident passed by harmlessly. The bus came, I boarded it, and was carried on towards my hotel, glancing behind at Renguang as we pulled out into the traffic, sad at leaving him, as he walked back home. I have never seen him since. I then simply sought to be faithful to him, relaying to colleagues in Hong Kong the contents of his requests for help. And now I seek also to be faithful to him, by relaying to you his request that he and others like him might be heard by you.

★★★★★★★★★★★★★★★★

"Be a reporter for us". The words remained with me for the rest of the evening, and for the rest of my time in China. Indeed they have done so since, even to this day. That is why I am writing this book.

I do not claim to be more than one observer of the China scene — there are others who know much more than I do. Indeed to some of them, close friends and colleagues, I remain deeply indebted for their wisdom, vision and insight. This book, if they will, is as much theirs in that sense as mine! It has been my privilege to work with most of the main evangelical China ministries in one way or another, especially the Hong Kong based ones.

But I do claim that God spoke to me that night in Shanghai, and laid a commission upon me to serve the Christians in China by helping others in other lands and other churches to hear their heartcry. Perhaps this book may help someone for the first time to hear that cry, or to understand it more clearly before the Lord. Or perhaps, through the words of this "reporter", someone will know more clearly that there is a voice of God's people in China to which they have been partly deaf or unclear up to this point. If that is so, then the task of preparing this book will have been well worth while.

This book is not a scholarly treatise; it is not a well-documented presentation. Cries that come from the heart rarely are. I trust, then, that you will accept and receive it for what it is — a heartcry.

CHAPTER 2

CRY FROM THE FIELDS

A few years and many miles on from my time with the Chens in Shanghai, I shared a meal in the home of another couple in church leadership in Southern China. I shall call them Zhang. We ate a magnificent meal — in stark contrast to the very basic accommodation in which they lived. We chatted happily and animatedly about the work in which they were engaged and about the church in their area of China.

Brother Zhang shared something that must seem very odd to many of us who are used to meeting as believers more or less whenever and wherever we choose. "We never meet", he confided to me, "except that we have a back door to the room we meet in". Even in the late 1980's, before the troubles of 1989, they knew that they could be raided by the security police in their area, though there is no law in China that forbids house church activities. He shared that some of the children have become spiritually sensitive — they play outside the meeting places, and the Lord warns them if the security police are coming. They sense by the Spirit of God that there is danger. One tells another, and they go to the meeting place to warn those in there. Hence the "back door" — an escape route from an interrupted meeting!

I knew that these were serious things that he was sharing. He had spent twenty years in prison for his faith. He had been arrested for teaching the Scriptures to young people in the 1950's, betrayed by a leader in the Three Self Patriotic Movement (TSPM) church in which he had previously served the Lord.

It was, however, another comment from brother Zhang that hit home to me even harder. It came to me as a challenge from the Lord, as if the Lord Himself were speaking and not brother Zhang. While we were talking about the needs of the house churches in his area of China, he suddenly said: *"I have many young people who long to be able to serve Jesus effectively, but I cannot train them because I do not have the personnel or the materials to do so. I cannot send them to the TSPM theological seminaries, because the content is too political. Nor can I send them abroad, for to do so would mean that their records would be marked."*

★★★★★★★★★★★★★★★★

"Many young people". How evocative that phrase is in terms of China. There were "many young people" involved in the Cultural Revolution in the 60's and the early 70's. Patrick Johnstone has called them the "lost generation" youth for "the education and future of millions of young people were jeopardised by the madness of the Cultural Revolution". He assesses that most are now "sick of Marxism but have no life philosophy except self-gratification. Many have turned to crime." (Operation World). What a waste of such idealism and zeal. They gave their all for what the present leadership has now described as a "disaster".

There were "many young people" in the Tiananmen Square in May and June of 1989. They played out a carnival of high hopes for something new. Then they died as the protest was stamped out in vicious bloodshed. Chai Ling, the most prominent girl student leader, has spoken since the massacre of having sat beside a fifteen year old boy in the Square. He had already made out a will, and now, speaking for many, he mused on his life being like that of an insect beside him — so quickly obliterated by one quick or careless movement of a human hand or foot. How true that has been for thousands of China's prime young people in those awful events of June 1989.

What a challenge their zeal, their idealism, their willingness to pay a price presents to us. What if we could play our part to see it released for the Gospel? What a vision — to see that Red Guard revolutionary fervour redeemed by the blood of Jesus and released in an eternal and crucial cause — that of the Gospel of the Lord Jesus Christ in China.

★★★★★★★★★★★★★★★★

My own personal path to the Zhang's simple room that night, indeed my path to China, has been so very different. There was no Red Guard revolutionary zeal there! But there was a common link. It was when I was in that same age group — the "young people" age group — that God reached into my life, changing both me and my whole direction in life. I know from personal experience how critical was the age of those young people of which we talked that night. In retrospect, though there have been for me many steps along that path, I see three steps as being especially critical.

The first step for me was relatively simple. I needed to become a real Christian and God set about, in His love, dealing with that. I came to the Lord at the age of about 14 through Scripture Union camps. I can only say that around that time God had placed a hunger in my heart. That summer in the South of England I understood the Gospel clearly for the first time, and I

13

responded. From that point, I found that I knew the Lord Jesus. He was my Friend; the Bible, His word, was real. That has remained so from that day to this. The first and vital step on the road to China had been taken.

A few short years later I found myself at Cambridge University. After a rather shaky spiritual start there, Jesus in His mercy confronted me with the next two key steps that I needed to take. The second step had to do with the Lordship of Jesus in my life. He already was My Saviour. That had been settled in the first step which I had taken at the age of fourteen. But He wanted more — He wanted me!

In my third year at Cambridge I had become aware of the need to be filled with the Holy Spirit, and was seeking God about this. I knew that I needed to take practical steps. I had heard that David Watson, then a curate in a church at Cambridge, could help in the matter of the baptism in the Spirit. I therefore went to seek him out. The conversation we had took a rather unexpected turn. I was confronted by the Lordship of Jesus as much as by the promise of power. I knew now that Jesus wanted to be in charge of every area of my life.

The issue was a simple but costly one. At that time I had a girlfriend who was a Christian. Yet David challenged me with this question, "Does this girl help you or hinder you to walk with Jesus?" I had to be honest and say that she did not help me at all. David stated that, if I was serious about the matter of the Holy Spirit, I would need to obey God in the matter of my romantic attachments. There was nothing improper or immoral in the relationship. It was simply that it was not what God wanted. If I wanted more of Him, He was going to have to have more of me.

In retrospect it is clear to me that the Lord Jesus was using this matter as a sign of whether I wanted Jesus to be in charge of my life. This important choice I made was not easy, but in the final analysis I wanted my life to be completely surrendered to the will of God. I broke off the relationship, though I found it costly. If I had known what God had in store for me, both in terms of China and Christine, I would have obeyed more quickly and with less fuss. But, like any step of faith and obedience, I did not know at the time what blessing God was to bring about through it.

The next night I returned to David's house, and we prayed together, claiming the promise in Luke 11:13 regarding the Holy Spirit: "If you then who are evil know how to give good gifts to your children, how much more will your heavenly Father give the Holy Spirit to those who ask Him". David pointed out the meaning of the verse — the Holy Spirit was a gift from our loving heavenly Father; all I had to do was to claim that gift by faith. He seemed to feel that was easy, and that I needed simply to accept that God had heard us as we prayed together claiming the Luke 11:13 promise. For my part I did not think it was quite that simple. My problem was that I was still thinking about the girl friend, and was quite near to tears. I just was not in a praising mood.

After encouraging me, David graciously sent me away into the night. I walked down the back street in Cambridge in which he lived at the time. I was not aware of doing anything special, except setting out to go home to my digs. Not far from David's house, two things suddenly happened to me. Firstly, I became aware of the nearness and love of the Lord Jesus in a way that far surpassed anything that I had known in the seven years of my Christian life up till that point. Secondly, my Adam's apple, low down as I remained near to tears, suddenly became involved in a very different kind of activity. I observed that I was worshipping God in a new tongue — the gift that the Bible calls 'speaking in tongues'. I suppose there was one striking observation to make about the way that gift came — nobody who disagreed with that could blame me for it, because it did not seem to have anything to do with what I had been doing in the minutes previous to it happening. It was

God's gift to me! I knew that my loving heavenly Father had answered His promise in Luke 11:13. I had received the promise that the disciples were given in Acts 1:8.

The second step had been taken; I had experienced a new reality and power in my Christian life. A few months later I had the chance to go on a team taking Bibles into Russia. That would have been impossible before then. Now there was a new reality that enabled me to trust God — even crossing Russian borders with guards searching the vehicle in which we carried the Bibles.

But there was still one other matter on the agenda of God in that year at Cambridge. The third step concerned a call to China. On the face of it I was not a very likely candidate; I had no interest or background in mission in general or China in particular. The nearest thing to it had been an odd incident at a university Christian Union prayer meeting one lunchtime. An older gentleman, who was one of the advisers, was sitting in front of me. Without saying anything that I remember, he turned round, placed in my hands a magazine on missionary work in Asia, and turned back to the front again. I did not know why he had done that, for I had never spoken to him before. Nothing much seemed to come of it — I do not even know if I read the magazine at all carefully. But in retrospect it seems to have been the Lord's way of dropping a hint.

But now that I knew a little bit more about the power and reality of the Holy Spirit, God began to quicken the pace in this matter. Just a few weeks later I was admitted to hospital with appendicitis. I took with me a book entitled 'A Thousand Miles Of Miracle In China', which was the story of a missionary in China during the Boxer Rebellion. I never read any further than the preface to the book. But that alone spoke to me more than most of the books I have read. The author gave his reasons for being a missionary in China. He used a very simple illustration to make his point. "If you see ten men carrying a heavy pole," he asked, "and nine men are at

16

one end of the pole, and only one at the other, whom do you help?" With China's millions, and countless numbers of them passing into eternity without ever hearing the gospel of Christ, it seemed obvious to me that I needed to consider with great honesty the challenge to help the "one man" — the relatively few who serve China's church. How many cities in England or the USA or elsewhere have "the nine men at the other end of the pole"? How many have several or more good churches, so that Christians are spoilt for choice?

After the operation, while still in hospital, I happened to watch a programme on the television in my room about the Chinese and what they think about British people. I was very interested in the programme, having just read the preface to the book. To be honest, I had never given much thought at all to the Chinese. I cannot remember ever seeing one in Cambridge in the mid-sixties, nor were "Chinese takeaways" as common as they are now!

After the book and television programme there came a voice. A nurse, whom I cannot recollect having seen or talked to in the hospital before, came up to my bedside and simply said, "Have you ever thought of being a missionary to China?" I cannot remember speaking to her again. Nor have I any idea why she should have said what she did.

As I considered her words, it was as if God were speaking to me. "It is not her, but Me who is asking you that question." It was as though my life was a blank sheet of paper and God, who was in charge of my life, had written the word "China" on that piece of paper. I knew that God had spoken to me, and never doubted from that day forward that China was to be a major priority in my life.

I had never considered following such a path. China had never figured in my thoughts until this small series of events brought me to the realisation that God was quite clearly directing my thoughts and footsteps to that great nation. A couple of people had been faithful and done what God had prompted them to do. The elderly adviser at Cambridge had handed me a magazine about Asia. The nurse had confronted me with a straight question. From virtually nowhere, China had been pushed to the very front of my thinking.

I think that it would be fair to say that, since those two events in Cambridge, every decision of any importance in my life has been taken with China in mind — even my marriage to Christine! After Cambridge, I went to work with David Watson in York, as an unordained, unpaid, fulltime church worker — the first that David had in that exciting period. It seemed a good step to be further trained in church work. I was there from 1967 to 1969. But as I began to settle there, the Holy Spirit rebuked me one night, and told me that it was time to move on.

I went from there to Taiwan for ten years. I flew into the island in April 1969, without a missionary society behind me, without a secure income, without a job, without knowing anyone there but one couple to whom I had been introduced, but had never met. But I knew that God has said to go. The Lord took care of my every need. David's church in York stood behind me in finance for 10 years. As far as the job went, my problem became that I had too much to do, not too little. I was invited to work with Campus Evangelical Fellowship, a key student work on the island (the equivalent of UCCF or Inter-Varsity). I taught at the leading University on the island, National Taiwan University, growing close to key Chinese young people. I preached widely across a variety of denominations on the island. I was involved in frontline leadership of an Operation Mobilisation style village outreach work.

The ten years there were crucial to learning Chinese — both the language (Mandarin) and the people! I lived very close to the ground, without a missionary society, in a way that showed me much about their culture and approach to life — or perhaps showed me enough after 10 years to realise that I did not understand them very well at all! Given that China was in the totally closed period of the Cultural Revolution, it proved an excellent training and serving period.

In 1979, as China began to open up, Christine and I moved back to the UK. I planted a church in York, and we were involved in local pastoral work for a period of time. The relationship with Acomb Christian Fellowship has been a precious one for us, for there we found faithful Christians who would stand behind us in prayer — and often in fasting. Much of what God has opened up for China in the 1980's for me can be traced to the faithfulness of the praying men and women there.

In 1980 the Overseas Missionary Fellowship approached me and asked me to be the first China Coordinator that they had appointed for the UK. I held that position for 4 years — till 1984. It was another special period for me, pioneering that work. It gave me a unique opportunity for "total immersion" in the work that had grown out of the China Inland Mission under Hudson Taylor. There was an open door to key China ministries in China, Hong Kong and elsewhere that never would have come without OMF.

During that period unique opportunities came to see the China scene from many angles. I sat on the British Council of Churches China Study Project Committee and also on the BCC's own China Advisory Committee. I met with top Chinese church leaders from the Three Self Patriotic Movement and the China Christian Council. I sat with them in large gatherings, like the first major China conference in Montreal, Canada in 1981, where I was one of only a very small handful of evangelicals. I organised the meeting between the TSPM and evangelicals in 1982 in London, and sat on the BCC committee which, with Bishop Ding and three others from China, wrote the report on the TSPM visit that year to the United Kingdom. I even represented the only

19

(I believe) dissenting voice on the committee that drew up the BCC report to its general assembly on the visit of the Archbishop of Canterbury to China in 1983.

Yet at the same time I had full and exciting exposure to the other side. I was close to various key sources in Hong Kong that gave us the other side of the picture — the house church side. I travelled in and met with key house church leaders like the Chens, hearing the story from their side.

I do not want to discuss that tension between the TSPM and the house churches further at this point. That will be done in later chapters. I simply want to point out that I have had opportunity, as very, very few others outside of China have, to hear directly and firsthand from both sides. There are few that have been granted that opportunity by the Lord. What I therefore share with you in these pages is from deep personal experience and conviction.

In the second half of the 80's there has been for me a season of extensive practical ministry for China — for example, in radio work, together with Derek Prince Ministries and the Far Eastern Broadcasting Company. Then there have been tapes and books and other ministries, such as supplying prayer information, or helping professionals and others to serve China. I have travelled much in the Far East, the USA and occasionally in Europe, with diverse opportunities to share and preach. But running through it all has been a single thread — China.

★★★★★★★★★★★★★★★★★★★★★★★

My background differs widely from those young people that brother Zhang was talking about. Cambridge and the rest of it is in some ways a million miles from China. But there is a point of identification there. It was while I was a member of that group known as "young people" that God spoke into my life, turned me around, and sent me out to serve Jesus and China. I know what the Holy Spirit can do with the most unlikely people — like me — and I rejoiced then and now in the challenge that brother Zhang laid before me that day.

I rejoice in it for China and I rejoice in it for the nations outside of China. A close friend of mine, Ben Moore, has summed up the challenge that must come from the church to young people in our generation. Ben wrote: "I told the young people that the desires they have to do wild, crazy, different, scary, radical and exciting things are desires that have been placed there by God. They will either use these desires to be on risky and daring missions for God, or they will be lured by Satan into using these desires with drugs, illicit sex, and other forms of sin that are destructive to themselves and others. When I gave the invitation for them to give their lives now to the kingdom of God and its extension in the earth, I told them that they could move powerfully in God beginning right now. It was a hard message and a hard invitation."

But it was the message that brother Zhang was relaying to me on behalf of these young people. They had crossed that bridge. Now they wanted help to be trained to walk further down that path of obedience to the Lord Jesus Christ. Nobody needs to tell them that it involves "risky living" in China today.

What a challenge for me — and for you who read this book. If the radio work in which we are involved can help one Chinese to come to know the Lord and to be used by Him; or one Christian book enables a keen but untrained young Chinese Christian to serve the Lord Jesus better, then that is surely a prize worth praying, planning and battling for! Yet brother Zhang talked of many young people needing such help — not just one!

He does not stand alone in his cry for help to us. The church in China has always produced heroes of the faith, men like him, people about whom most Western Christians never hear a word. They have laboured

21

faithfully, suffered and persevered under the most extreme circumstances, and remain faithful to God and His word. And they continue to do so today, as unsure as we are about what each new turn of events in China will bring. They expect little in return for what they have given and done, but they are jealous for the work of God, and long to see the gospel reaching all parts of China.

Let me give a few extracts from letters that have reached us via such organisations as the Far Eastern Broadcasting Company, who labour faithfully and effectively to send radio broadcasts into China.

"I do not have a Bible. I want to ask you to get me one copy of the Bible, for I need it urgently...If I have a Bible I can read it to the other believers during the meetings, even if I can't explain it all... Please believe me, I will not let the Bible lie asleep in my home."

"I am not a man with much learning. My understanding of the Lord's truth is not profound. I have no spiritual books. However, the responsibility to pastor the believers in the village has been laid on me."

"I am 37 years old. I am a preacher in my church. I would like to devote myself to the Lord. I plead with you, though I know you are very busy...that no matter how busy you are, please try by every possible means to send us spiritual books, since our spiritual lives need your help."

"Since the opening for the gospel in 1979, the gospel of the Kingdom of Heaven has become more and more successful. The number of those saved grows every day. This is all the Holy Spirit's work. But our faith is insufficient, so we don't understand the truth contained in the Bible. We have been falling short of both God and man, and we are unable to satisfy the needs of the believers. Please pray often for us. I ask God to guide you not to forget the needs we face in our lives, since our spiritual lives are really thirsty and need your nurture and culture."

Although these letters may convey some lack of understanding, yet underneath them can be clearly heard the heartcry of people who long only to serve God with all that they have and are, and who desire desperately to see God's people fed spiritually and brought to maturity in Christ.

Behind the Bamboo Curtain a revival is taking place of astonishing proportions. The Holy Spirit is moving sovereignly across the land of China, sweeping people into the kingdom of God in their thousands, even millions. Because of this amazing growth in the church, a large proportion of believers are without Bibles, teaching materials or training of any consistent nature. They are experiencing a famine that will never capture the world's headlines, but which is just as real to them as the desperate physical plight of so many lands on the African continent. They are starving spiritually because of the lack of the word of God. They are desperate to be able to read a Bible and to hear it expounded. One itinerant evangelist went with some fellow believers to the countryside to evangelise. As soon as it became known in the area that they had arrived, people came from miles around, some walking day and night, so that they could attend an evening meeting that was scheduled to last a couple of hours. When the preacher had finished what he had to say, they begged him to continue so that they could hear more of God's word. They were not prepared to let him eat or sleep, or do so themselves, in order to take full advantage of the opportunity to digest 'spiritual food'.

This example is typical of so many situations in Mainland China. There is an incredible hunger among many of God's people there for spiritual nourishment. A friend of mine who travels regularly into China was invited to speak to preachers in a certain province. When he arrived at the home where he was to minister, he was met by 140 key preachers and co-workers from 10 different districts in the province. Some of them had cycled 150 kilometres to be there, and several had been on the road for a day or more. He preached and prayed for them from early morning until late at night, with only two short breaks for meals.

As soon as the meeting had ended at 11pm, he was put into the front seat of a large truck and driven some 20 kilometres to the next village to speak to a whole new group. After some sleep, the next ministry session began with prayer at 5.30am. The evening meeting finished at 11pm, and although there were supposed to be only 150 people present, more and more arrived throughout the day, crowding out the rooms of the house, standing at the doorway and looking in through the window. They remained there for hours on end listening to what this servant of God had to say. One memory remains in my mind of his description of one such occasion. He observed that the hungry believers were packed in so tightly that they were actually sitting on his feet while he was preaching to them!

The longing to receive sound teaching and instruction in the word of God is so great that no obstacle seems too hard to overcome — if it results in a meeting where the Scriptures will be expounded. Such believers fear heresy and wrong belief. They literally seize any opportunity given to them to learn that truth of the Bible from those with more understanding than they have.

★★★★★★★★★★★★★★★★

In 1968 I had the opportunity to take Christian literature into Czechoslovakia. At the time the church was enjoying considerable freedom under the liberal policies of Alexander Dubcek. We were allowed to hold a young peoples' camp in the mountains that summer, teaching the word of God to the young people who came, and generally to enjoy our time with the young Christians of that country. The atmosphere was good and relatively easy-going and we took advantage of it. I can remember a Czech pastor saying to me, as he saw the opportunities for sharing the Gospel and for building up the believers, that it had been twenty years since he had seen or known such a time of freedom and opportunity for the church in Czechoslovakia.

One fateful day, however, everything changed. The Russian tanks rolled aggressively over Czechoslovakia's borders, and Dubcek's administration came to an abrupt end. The door was shut, the borders were tightened up, and a very hard season began for the church in that land. Nothing was as it had been during those few short months of freedom for Christian activity. So quickly can a situation change in a nation.

China has experienced a thawing in its relations with other countries, and a considerable relaxing in the tight grip that prevailed over people in the country, and especially in the church, up to 1976. There is a partially open door through which tourists can go to visit this great land, and which professionals can use if they wish to work in China and serve its people in their chosen field. It is also a door which Christians can utilise in various other ways. Just how long the door will remain ajar is impossible to say, particularly after the events of June 1989. The lesson of Czechoslovakia in 1968 must not be forgotten. That lesson is simple, and this is it: *if the door to such a land is even partly open, then the church of Jesus Christ outside must help those inside in any way that they request, and they must help them swiftly.*

If they articulate needs to us, then we must respond to those needs. We should not wait, nor put it on the agenda for some unspecified period in the future. The reason for that is simple — we do not know if there will be a future like the present time. We need to act now, and if the door should close later, we may have all the time we want for meditative inaction on the subject!

The June 1989 events in Tiananmen Square should only serve to make us more aware of the urgency of those needs in China. As I write this, in the same month as the Tiananmen massacre took place, I do not know what the effect will be on the church. Nor do I know whether the government of Li Peng is a temporary or long-term phenomenon. If it is to be long-term, then I suspect there will be hard times ahead for the church in China. But surely that is a challenge to do more, and more quickly, about the work of responding to their heartcry.

We must make full use of the opportunity while it is there. Policies in China have been known to swing violently from one extreme to another on many occasions. We have seen that vividly on our television screens and in our newspapers. A yet more radical shift in the general mood of its leaders could see the door to China close just as quickly as it did in Czechoslovakia in 1968.

Many people saw the present open door policy of China as God's answer to prayer. Having prayed it open, dare we ignore it when we have the resources to meet many of the needs of our brethren? Having seen God turn the events of China's history once in recent years, will we not seek God to do it again, and to open the door wider than it has yet been? I pray that it will be so. And now that open door is partly closed, may God help us to grasp the urgency of the hour, and consider carefully how we can be involved in influencing and serving the people of that land.

★★★★★★★★★★★★★★★★

John Angell James was a man burdened for China more than a hundred years ago. He saw the opportunity and the challenge to Christians outside China to take spiritual advantage of the open door and to help China's church. He had a long-standing friendship with Robert Morrison, one of the great early pioneers (in every sense of that word) of the foreign involvement of the work of Christ in China. James had already organised an appeal to send a million New Testaments to China through the

26

British and Foreign Bible Society. The appeal was so successful that twice that number — two million New Testaments — had been sent to China. So James was not given to theory in the matter of serving China's church.

In 1858, the year before he died, James penned these words: "The conversion of China is, one way or other, the business of every Christian upon earth — and every Christian upon earth can do something for it and ought to do what he can. The man who says 'What have I to do with this matter?' is either ignorant, indolent or covetous and is altogether heartless towards the cause of Christ. He that says 'What concern have I in China's conversion?' just asks the question 'What fellowship have I with Christ?' We are all too apt to think of what the church can do and ought to do and not what we individually can do and ought to do, and either through modesty, timidity or avarice, lose ourselves and our individual obligations in the crowd. Do you then ask whose business the conversion of China is, I answer, 'yours, whosoever you are who may read this page. Yours', I say, 'as truly as that of any other man on the face of the earth'. Here it is, I offer it to you, and in the Name of Christ bid you take it. Take it into your hand, your heart, your purse, your closet — you dare not refuse it!"

Perhaps we find that kind of language and challenge a trifle strong. Should it today not be even stronger, given the massive population growth in China and the corresponding growth in spiritual need? Dare we say the words are any less relevant today? For they do have their modern equivalents, voices now from within China that give the same message in another form: *"I have many young people who long to be able to serve Jesus effectively, but I cannot train them because I do not have the personnel or the materials to do so."*

27

CHAPTER 3

THE RED SUN RISES

This chapter is intended to provide a brief overview of the historical events that have led to the present day. It is deliberately slanted towards the way that events have affected the church and the Christians in China, for it is with them that we are concerned. This is not intended to be a comprehensive historical analysis — others have done that with great skill, and their books are available.

Although the history of Christianity in China dates from the seventh century, this summary will only deal with the nineteenth and twentieth centuries. The history of China over these two centuries is one of turmoil, upheaval, violence, uprisings, bloodshed and human suffering on an unprecedented scale. This is the backdrop against which China's current dramas are being played out.

The 19th Century

As trade routes were being opened into and through China in the early years of the nineteenth century, the first Protestant missionaries set foot on Chinese soil. Among the first pioneers was Robert Morrison

(1782-1834) who was sent out by the London Missionary Society. His activities were confined to the Macao and Canton district but, by translating the Bible between 1807 and 1819, he laid a solid foundation for those who followed.

The 1841 Opium War led to the colonisation of Hong Kong by the British and the opening up of five Treaty Ports to foreign trade and foreign residency. While these developments made China accessible to foreign missionaries, millions of lives were lost and destroyed through the use of opium that was forcibly taken into China by the colonial powers of the so-called civilised world. While the seeds of the gospel could now be sown freely in China, other seeds were being sown which would result in a bitter harvest in the troubled years to follow. The Chinese people had much to endure from foreign exploitation and interference, and a fierce undercurrent of resentment and anger was being generated.

The latter half of the nineteenth century was marked by conflict between rival warlords, who controlled the various provinces of China. It also saw sporadic rebellion against the Dynastic rulers. Between 1851 and 1864, the Manchu Dynasty resisted the Taiping Rebellion. Wholesale slaughter accompanied the crushing of this movement which had been led by a man with pseudo-Christian aspirations of a new puritan age.

Despite these troubles, Protestant Missionary activity was on the increase. J. Hudson Taylor (1832-1905), who founded the China Inland Mission in 1865, and his colleagues were breaking new ground in the interior provinces. By the end of the century, there were reckoned to be over 110,000 Protestants and almost half a million Roman Catholics in China. One result of this growing Christian influence was the development of schools, colleges and hospitals. A new generation of educated Chinese people was emerging.

Dr Sun Yatsen (1867-1925), the son of a Christian

convert, was a product of the new education system. He practised as a doctor in Macao but turned his attention to politics and became involved in revolutionary agitation against the Manchu Dynasty. He fled to the West in 1895 after being involved in a failed insurrection but was destined to return in 1911 as the first President of a new Republic.

The nineteenth century ended with continuing unrest in China. Feelings of resentment and hatred against the colonial powers, which had been simmering for so long, were reaching boiling point.

CHINA — 1900 to 1919.

The twentieth century dawned with the Empress Dowager, Tzu Hsi, encouraging the Boxer uprising. In a tide of nationalistic fervour, about 32,000 Chinese Christians were slain along with 235 Protestant missionaries and Roman Catholic priests. However, the final outcome was that the Chinese people suffered further humiliation as allied forces invaded and took control. More land was lost to foreign ownership and control as retribution was exacted on the Chinese people.

In the immediate aftermath of the Boxer rebellion, Christian missions continued to prosper and the ethnic minorities, as well as the Han people, were touched by the gospel in the farthest corners of China.

In 1911, another revolt broke out against the Manchu Dynasty but, unlike some previous insurrections, it was led by educated men who were riding high on a spirit of nationalism. Dr Sun Yatsen returned from exile to lead the Kuomintang party and the revolution was successful. The Manchu Dynasty came to an end. The new leaders of China were nearly all products of Christian schools.

Regrettably, Sun Yatsen had to give way to Yuan Shihkai, the commander of what was then the only effective military force in China. It soon became evident that Yuan wanted to be a dictator and the Kuomintang party, despite dominating the new parliament, had little influence over the military executive. Civil war broke out in 1913 and, after Yuan's death in 1916, a power vacuum was left at national level. Democratic government had failed to bring order to a China which had traditionally been ruled by those with the most guns. Events in Russia in 1917 cast a shadow over China. Political thought also had began to take a harder line. Leaders like Sun Yatsen had begun to look to Moscow and the Bolsheviks for an answer rather than to the democratic systems of the old colonial powers.

The First World War and the subsequent betrayal of China to Japan by the Western powers shook the faith of many intellectuals in the moral superiority of the West and of Christianity. China had been on the side of the Allies during the war. Once the war had ceased, she expected the territory held by Germany to be given back to her. When the Treaty of Versailles was concluded, however, it was left in the hands of the Japanese who had captured it from Germany during the war.

The May 4th Movement of 1919, which was a dominant influence in the minds of the 1989 student leaders, sprang out of this. Intellectuals in China marched in orderly fashion to the centre of Peking (Beijing), proclaiming the need for the Chinese government to stand with more strength and dignity against the unjust conditions of the Treaty of Versailles.

These events did the cause of Christianity a great deal of harm, as it was inextricably linked with imperialism in the minds of many intellectuals and others. As a result, many of the intelligentsia turned to scientific humanism or Marxism. Left-wing students and thinkers founded an anti-Christian movement. The movement was a signal that the growing influence of Communism would be accompanied by persecution of Chinese believers.

CHINA — 1920 to 1949.

Hopes of a new society were kindled in the hearts of some in 1921 when the Chinese Communist Party was established in Shanghai with the assistance of the Communist International (Comintern). Mao Tsetung was among the twelve founding members. Under the leadership of Li Dazhao, the first Chinese Marxist, and Chen Duxiu, the new party set itself the goal of seizing power in China.

At first, the Communists and the Kuomintang worked together. Chiang Kaishek, who had emerged as military leader of the Republic after the death of Sun Yatsen, had visited Russia and appeared impressed by Soviet ideas. His successful military campaigns in the North brought some order to China in 1927. However the emerging power struggle between the two parties was beginning to take the form of violent conflict.

1927 also saw several abortive attempts at armed insurgency by the Communist Party in different cities. As a result of these early setbacks, the years after that saw a change of tactics. More emphasis was placed on peasant-based insurgency in south-central China with the use of guerrilla warfare. Mao Tsetung was a keen advocate of this new strategy. During this period he moved up the ranks of the Chinese Communist Party (CCP). His role lay in the development of these ideas with specific application to the Chinese situation.

Against this backdrop of internal strife and guerilla warfare within the nation, Christian missions suffered a period of severe persecution in the late 1920s. Large numbers of missionaries had to take refuge in the cities and many returned to their homelands. The 1930's saw a reversal of this trend, with some semblance of normality returning.

During this period the Nationalists held a position of strength because of their superiority in numbers. It became obvious to the Communists that, if they were to survive, they would have to increase their forces. They therefore made a strategic withdrawal to the mountains in the North-West of the country, a journey by foot of 6,000 miles. The Long March, as it has come to be known, took from 1934 until 1936. The Communists suffered many casualties as a result of attacks by the Nationalist forces, but this feat is still held in high regard by the Chinese. Indeed many of the present (now geriatric) leadership have tended to use their presence on the march as a qualification — or a mandate — to lead today. It stands to them as almost a guarantee of Marxist orthodoxy. Certainly, at the time it inspired many young people to join the Communist forces. There can be no doubt that the impact of this event was deep and lasting.

In 1937 Japan attacked China. Japan, that other great Eastern nation, was more militarily orientated than now it seems. It had taken Manchuria and was threatening China. The Communist and Nationalist forces stood uneasily together against the threat of invasion, but the Japanese were eventually defeated by the Allies at the end of the Second World War.

When the Japanese surrendered in 1945, the Communist armies found themselves in a strategic position to accept the surrender. At that key point in history, the Nationalist forces led by Chiang Kaishek were in West China, far away from that historical event.

Mao was by this time firmly established as leader of the Communists. They had gained more and more popular support, partly through stepping up their efforts for reorganisation and reform of local government, taxation and agrarian policy in the areas under their control. They had also earned much popular support by the conduct of their troops. The general discipline of their men led to an unusually low incidence of plundering or civilian abuse in the rural communities through which they passed. This discipline obviously made an impact on a largely peasant population who well knew what it was to be abused.

After the Japanese surrender, Mao met with Chiang Kaishek in Chungking to negotiate China's future, but the failure of the talks led to a resumption of civil war.

34

From 1946 until 1949, bitter warfare was waged. The armies clashed head on and millions of lives were lost. The smaller but better organised Communist forces slowly gained the upper hand. The Nationalist forces were numerically superior, but their poor morale and other shortcomings resulted in their defeat and exile from Mainland China. Chairman Mao, the now victorious leader over Japanese and Nationalist enemy alike, stood up in Tiananmen Square, where so much of China's history has been written. To a vast crowd representing a nation that largely welcomed him, he proclaimed victory — over external oppressors of every kind. To a Chinese people so abused, not the least by Western and other foreign powers, he spoke a sentiment that caused many Chinese hearts to leap for joy — China had stood up at last; the Chinese people had come of age. They were determined that they would never again be dominated, raped and plundered.

TAIWAN — 1949-1989.

The beleaguered Kuomintang forces took refuge on Taiwan (Formosa), an island some 90 miles off the South-East Coast of China. Taiwan now became the base for Chiang Kaishek and the defeated Nationalist army and officials. Even today the Nationalist descendants of Chiang Kaishek on the island of Taiwan claim to be the true government of China in exile in Taipei, the capital city, waiting for the opportunity to liberate Mainland China from the Communists. They call themselves "The Republic of China", as opposed to Beijing's "People's Republic of China", making the point (which both sides agree on) that Taiwan remains only a province of China, not a state in its own right.

The issue behind that agreement of the two sides regarding the island is as obvious as it is controversial — of which China is Taiwan a province? Until the 1970's, with USA backing, Taiwan held the China seat in the United Nations. In recent years, however, with Mainland

China's emergence from the almost total obscurity of the period of the Cultural Revolution (1966-1976), Beijing has taken over that place — as well as the Olympic and many other such international "China" seats. Meanwhile, the people of Taiwan, hardworking and skilled in every form of industry and commerce, have developed an economic base of remarkable proportions — they rank as one of the "four tigers" of Asia (along with Singapore, Hong Kong and South Korea), placed behind the economic leader of the pack — Japan.

Taiwan faces its own tensions internally and externally to this day. Internally, parts of the population have never fully accepted their Mainland brothers taking over the island in 1948-49. The original Taiwanese population can be divided into two streams in general terms, though there are many more smaller streams and eddies. Firstly, there are the indigenous tribes or "mountain" peoples, who could in some remarkable ways be likened to the North American Red Indians. They are Polynesian in origin, rather than pure ethnic Chinese. Secondly, there are the ethnic Han Chinese who had come over from South East China in various waves during the course of the past several centuries. These are the "Taiwanese" peoples who were there long before Chiang Kaishek came, the more militant of whom see themselves as belonging to an Island state of Taiwan, not to China. There has been much tension and some bloodshed over the years on that issue.

On the international and external front the Taiwanese\Republic of China leadership also has to walk a difficult road. They must keep their economic bandwagon rolling — which they have done to this point with almost unbelievable skill and ability. Each new recession, each new wave of international economic or political pressures, seems only to draw from them deeper levels of ingenuity and ability. Sectors of the island's population are now incredibly wealthy, though that has brought social problems of a deep and increasingly insoluble nature.

Yet at the same time Taiwan needs to look to the future. Mainland China has never deviated from its avowed intention of reclaiming the Province of Taiwan as part of its own, nor has it renounced the use of force in the pursuit of that goal. Indeed, it is likely that the USA's close relationship and clear military commitment to Taiwan in the decades of the 1950's and 1960's was a major factor in frustrating Beijing's desire to regain Taiwan. The Island of Jinmen (literally "Golden Door", often known as Quemoy), situated right off the coast of China's Fujian Province, remains still in Taiwan's hands. It is a military fortress.

Despite this long history of declared mutual hostility, recent years have seen a new development — that of cautious rapprochement between the two Chinas. From early 1988, for the first time since 1949, the Taiwan government permitted its citizens to return to China. The condition was that they had to have relatives there — not that difficult a task for most of them! It seems that both sides welcomed the lessening of tensions. Both sides, as Chinese, are economic opportunists, so that there was significant growth in trade between them — entirely unofficially, of course, given the technical state of war. It is mostly done through Hong Kong.

However, Hong Kong's uneasy run-up to 1997, now explosively volatile following the June 1989 Tiananmen massacre, is watched with intense interest from the Taiwan side. There are of course parallels, given China's claim to both Hong Kong's and Taiwan's territory. Taiwan's first reaction to the massacre has been instinctive — for the first time since 1949 they have allowed their citizens to write and phone directly to Mainland China. But their reason is not what it seems — they simply want their people to give information about the Li Peng brutality to their relatives on the Mainland, so that the Communist savagery should not be concealed by the total news blackout and disinformation that has taken place in China. They want to deny the immediate Beijing version of the events — that no students died in Tiananmen. That version is now believed by many Chinese in other cities in China, whose only source of information is the official government media. But Taiwan's long-term reaction needs to be awaited — they are capable of cutting right back to the cold war period of hostilities as long as the "hardliners" remain in power in Beijing.

CHINA: 1949-1989.
THE STATE AND THE CHURCH.

Period 1. 1949-1966. Consolidation by the Marxists.

Following their total victory on the Mainland, the Communists held the first meeting of the People's Political Consultative Council in September 1949. As we have seen above, on October 1st Mao proclaimed the foundation of the People's Republic of China from Tiananmen — the gate of the Forbidden City in Beijing.

A new day had dawned in the history of China, but Mao had no intention of letting the country settle down and rehabilitate in a peaceful manner after the horrors of the preceding years. Anti-Communists were rooted out or slaughtered in a series of reprisals. The landlord class were special targets for Mao's attention, and it is estimated that just under one million people lost their lives, with all their land being given to the peasants.

Hatred towards their enemies and the use of violence against them were lessons that the Chinese Communists had learned well from Marxism-Leninism. Two of Mao's much-used catchphrases reflect that — "political power grows out of the barrel of a gun" and "doing revolution is not like going to a tea party."

Having won the hearts of the people, the next phase of Mao's strategy was the introduction of thought-reform. Chinese people of all ages, whether in or out of school, had to undergo self-criticism sessions and join Marxism-Leninism study groups. Mao believed that by using such methods — purging people of their old ways of thinking — he could create a new Communist person. Such a person would show absolute loyalty to the Party and the cause of revolution, would have a natural inclination to do good and would be creative, unselfish. They would be more interested in the corporate than the individual good.

What a contrast exists there with the Biblical truth that fallen man can only change through the redeeming work and changing power released for us by the Lord Jesus on the cross. No wonder many Christians in China faced a tough choice — to accept Mao's unrealistic humanist dogma or to hold to their Biblical faith (and be seen as anti-patriotic and anti-Party).

Communism demands absolute loyalty from its people. To achieve this, however, it must control the people's thoughts and motivations. An automatic conflict arises between Communism and Christianity, a conflict between atheism and theism. Atheism is basic to Communist dogma, ruling out completely any thought of the supernatural. It denies the deity of Christ, therefore, and any suggestion of the salvation afforded to mankind by His death and resurrection. The possibility that human beings are more then just physical — that they might have an eternal soul — is totally disregarded, as is life after death or future judgment. It denies the existence of an eternally valid moral law. I believe that that kind of thinking — man as matter only, without eternity in his soul — lies behind the ongoing Chinese low view of the value of human life.

Marx had little time for religion. He saw it as hindrance to the socialist revolution, something which had to be rooted out and destroyed. Lenin was even more forceful in his denunciations of anything to do with religion: "The roots of modern religion are deeply embedded in the social oppression of the working masses and in their apparently complete helplessness before the blind forces of capitalism. Fears created the gods. Every religious idea, every idea of a god, is an unspeakable abomination, a most repulsive infection."

Thus 're-education' and 're-moulding' are then obviously important tactics of the Communist Party in handling religious people, including Christians. In fact Christianity was singled out as a major target for vigorous attack in China, not only because it was considered to be anti-scientific, but also because it was identified with imperialist exploitation of the country.

On the surface it might seem that religious freedom is available in China. If we jump briefly over the years from the early period (pre-1966) that we are now discussing to today, we can see that it has now evolved into Article 36 of the Constitution. This states that "citizens of the People's Republic of China enjoy freedom of religious belief. No state organ, public organisation, or individual may compel citizens to believe in, or not to believe in any religion; nor may they discriminate against citizens who believe in or do not believe in any religion. The state protects normal religious activities. No-one can make use of religion to engage in activities that disrupt public order, impair the health of citizens or interfere with the educational system of the state. Religious bodies and religious affairs are not to be subject to any foreign domination."

At first glance that article of the Constitution does allow freedom of religion. A deeper understanding, however, reveals that much of the phraseology is open to interpretation. Certainly such freedoms are not be the same as we understand it in many other countries today. In Chinese Communist terms it is a temporary concession of the Party and the state to religious believers, permitting them either to believe or not believe in a certain religion. The State does not only offer to protect "normal religious activities". It also defines for its citizens which activites are to be considered as "normal". That definition is in strong ideological

40

hostility to Scripture. Communists believe religion will disappear from society at some point in time, through the joint forces of education and revolution. People will be freed from these archaic superstitions through socialist revolution. Eventually religion will, like a tree that is not tended, wither and die.

We need now to apply the historical and theoretical understanding of the Communist approach to religion that I have given in this section to the church in the 1950's. In the years leading up to the Marxist Liberation — the first half of the 20th century — there had been a steady increase in the number of Chinese people professing faith in Christ. There was therefore every reason to be optimistic about the future of Christianity in China. Christians held positions of importance in educational and government institutions and were actively involved in social reforms and literacy campaigns. The Christian missions were playing an important part through their medical and educational facilities, as well as their publishing programmes. By 1949 there were a large number of universities, schools and hospitals operated by missions and churches.

The Chinese church, though by no means flourishing, was at least beginning to take root and grow in genuinely Chinese soil. It was producing some Chinese preachers and evangelists with powerful ministries, men who have become known in the West for their contribution to the cause of the gospel. These included John Sung, the 'Flaming Evangelist', through whom countless numbers were won to Christ and Wang Mingdao, who stood for adherence to the Scriptures and withstood heresies and false teachings. Watchman Nee is perhaps the best known outside of China. His in-depth, systematic study of the Bible has brought many Christians to a clear understanding of the work of Christ in their lives. These and many others were taking responsibility for the growing Church in China, which was well down the road to becoming totally indigenous.

Once the Communists had taken over, however, all religious institutions were expected to obey the Party line and support the new United Front Policy. Many church buildings and other buildings associated with the work of the church, such as schools and hospitals, were taken over by the authorities.

In 1950, a document was published entitled 'Christian Manifesto', in which all missionaries were branded as imperialists. This being the ultimate accusation in China, strong pressure was therefore applied to Chinese Christians to request their missionary colleagues to withdraw from church work. By 1952, almost all of the missionaries had left China.

The new regime, under Mao, promised equality and social justice for all. Many young Christians began to feel that the Chinese Communist Party did perhaps have the answers to many of the problems facing China. As a result they gave up their faith — or considerably compromised it biblically — and became a part of the new order, sometimes in the process accepting the atheistic ideology of the government.

Some Christians tried to divide their loyalties between the Church and the Party. They struggled to support a government which on the one hand seemed to promote equality and social justice and on the other believed in and promoted atheism.

A campaign was at this point initiated in the church to root out all who were were accused of infection by the 'imperialist poison'. In 1952, Watchman Nee was arrested and was never released. In 1953 the Jesus Family was disbanded. 1955 saw the arrest of Wang Mingdao, a church leader who had refused to compromise with the State and stood against any political control of the church. He had, however, no forbidden relationships whatsoever with foreign missions. He was still arrested and accused in a nationwide accusation programme. Wang was not released until 1978. Christians and non-Christians alike had to undergo daily indoctrination and re-education programmes.

In 1956 Mao launched a new initiative, known as the Hundred Flowers Movement, which was an invitation to all intellectuals to express freely their ideas and give their criticisms of government policy. The resultant deluge of criticism so shocked Party officials that massive repression followed together with a further attack on intellectuals. Many of them were deported to remote parts of the country, some never to be seen again. Among them were many Christians. The policy of open criticism came to an abrupt end. Any criticism of the government came to be regarded as an act of treason.

Another of Mao's policies which proved to be a complete disaster was the Great Leap Forward in 1958. The land that had been given to the peasants was taken back from them to establish communes. Mao's plan was to turn China into a huge industrial-agricultural nation. Part of this plan was to divide up families and send them to different parts of China to form communes — which sometimes could be as large as several towns. This policy failed miserably. As the result of both severe flooding and drought, famine ensued. It is estimated that around thirty million Chinese peasants perished at this time.

All of this signalled a tentative and discouraging end to this first period of post-Liberation China. The period had begun with such high expectations for most of China. It had clearly brought some economic and social benefit. The cost of that benefit, however, was the same catalogue of injustice and suffering — especially to biblical Christians.

Period 2. 1966–76. The Cultural Revolution.

The failures at the end of the first period cast a shadow over Mao. In a real sense they can be seen at the cause of the second period — the Cultural Revolution. Within the confines of Party walls Mao had come in for some very strong criticism. The architect of the Communist victory of 1949 was not to be deterred, however. He responded In 1966 with a plan to revive the revolutionary fervour of the Party.

The Cultural Revolution was part of Mao's theory of permanent revolution and struggle, intended to give every new generation a chance to experience the meaning of revolution for itself. It was his belief that cultural revolution should be repeated continually — if necessary, as often as every seven or eight years. Mao went directly to the youth of the nation, inciting the teenage Red Guards to take revolutionary action against the Party and State bureaucracy. All schools were closed, and the Red Guards encouraged to take to the road, opposing and destroying everything that vaguely smelled of capitalism. The result was the almost complete breakdown of the institutions of government.

In political terms, the Cultural Revolution was supposed to rid the Party of 'rightist pragmatism', 'bourgeois tendency' and 'Soviet revisionism', in order to keep the flame of revolution alive. However, it quickly became a personality cult, with the Red Guards completely dedicated to Chairman Mao. Many will recall the scenes, inside and outside of China, of young Chinese waving the 'Thoughts of Chairman Mao', the famous little red book, and reciting its contents from memory.

Following that initial explosion of revolutionary fervour, there followed a second phase of the Cultural Revolution. This period saw millions of young people, intellectuals and Party and state workers from all levels (known as cadres) sent to the countryside to 'learn from the peasants'. As a result of this vast influx of people into the rural areas, agriculture was placed under a great strain. The 'peasants' despised the 'students' because they were a tremendous drain on the resources of the land, doing very little to add substantially to its productivity.

The higher educational system ceased to function until

1973. It did not begin to recover until around 1977. A whole generation of young people were unable to complete their education as a result. At the time revolutionary fervour was regarded as more than adequate to compensate for any lack of expertise. Scientific research stopped for a whole decade. Industry declined and urban residents suffered as they were hit with one political campaign after another.

Turning to the effects of all of this on the church, we may observe that once more Christians became a prime target for the zealous Red Guards. Church buildings were closed and confiscated; Bibles and Christian literature were destroyed; some Christians were publicly humiliated, assaulted physically and emotionally and even martyred for their faith. Leaders and church workers were forbidden to preach and many were sent to labour camps, factories or farms. Some Christians were driven to such depths of despair that they committed suicide. At one point in the Cultural Revolution period, there was no church or chapel open throughout China — Shanghai alone had had 200 such buildings by the 1950's. For a time religion was declared totally illegal. Christians dared not even so much as greet one another when they met.

There has always been two different philosophical approaches within Chinese Marxism to this question of religion. On the one hand, Premier Zhou Enlai, representing the 'moderates', believed that religion would eventually be rejected by a socialist society. He felt that education of the people would be sufficient to rid them of their religious beliefs. On the other hand, the Red Guards, representing the 'hardliners', wanted to obliterate Christianity completely and as quickly as possible. Their persecution of the church saw institutionalised Christianity disappear from the life of China.

During this dark time the faith and loyalty of many Christians to each other was put under the most extreme

45

test. Some betrayed Christ and their fellow Christians. As a result the fear of betrayal led to distrust even amongst the most godly Christians. Despite the onslaught by the Red Guards, however, the hidden church survived in one form or another, even spreading to areas where previously there had been no Christian witness, largely because believers had been exiled to scattered parts of the country.

The Christians devised ways and means of meeting, mostly in very small groups and in homes. Although the outward, public activities of the church were severely impeded, the Holy Spirit was not. He continued to move in great power, with many people being saved, healed and delivered — including Red Guards who could not help but be impressed by the lifestyle of the people they were persecuting.

That the Red Guards went too far was acknowledged by all, even by Mao himself. Eventually the army had had to be called in to restore some semblance of order. Mao's image was thus dealt a further heavy blow, one from which he never fully recovered. His Red Guards were either sent home or to work on communes in disgrace. Many of them felt they had been used and discarded, having wasted the most important years of their youth. They became disillusioned and mistrusting of the Party and even of the Communist cause itself.

Throughout the early 1970s, Premier Zhou Enlai made strategic efforts to limit the damage caused by the Cultural Revolution. At a Party meeting held in 1975 he proposed the 'Four Modernisations' of agriculture, industry, science and technology, and defence. The purpose of these modernisations was to bring China up to the standards of the West by the year 2000. In charge of the programme was Deng Xiaoping — who then, after the death of Zhou Enlai in 1976, was himself purged, having all of his posts taken away from him by the radicals.

The central core of the radicals had became known as

the Gang of Four, led by Mao's wife Jiang Qing. They in turn fell from power when they were arrested one month after the death of Mao Tsetung in 1976. These events signalled the end of the second post-Liberation period, that of the Cultural Revolution. It had been more than a decade of terrible turmoil in China, one in which most Christians suffered very deeply.

Period 3. 1976 – The Present Day.

The death of Mao saw the end of an era. His effective successor, Deng Xiaoping, with his great ability to survive setback and counter-attack, came back into power in 1977. Deng quickly made the Four Modernisations that had been introduced by Zhou Enlai his priority. Some desperate surgery was required on China's ailing economy, which had seen very little progress for twenty years.

Agriculture was the first area to which Deng turned his attention under the Four Modernisations programme. He was shrewd enough to realise that if people profit personally in some way from work that they are undertaking, they are more likely to be motivated to greater productivity. Thus his reform of agriculture centred around the peasants' self interest, rather than any revolutionary theories. An individual, a household, or a group of people would be allocated an increased plot of land to work, under contract to the State. The land would still belong to the State, but after the people working the land had turned in their alloted amount of produce to the State, at State prices, any surplus could be sold off at higher prices.

The rural reforms proved to be amazingly successful. After twelve consecutive years of loss, in 1979 the State farms were able to announce an overall profit. On the other hand, the urban reforms proved to be much more of a challenge, for the industrial economy was far more complex than the rural. The overall aim of the reforms was to replace the old system of direct control by the

State with a system that integrated planning and the market.

This programme of reforms encountered many difficulties and suffered not a few setbacks up to the climactic Tiananmen events of 1989. But despite the problems, China was then still firmly set in the direction of greater reforms. Naturally for China, these reforms have not taken place without some grave concern, and even opposition, by certain sections of the leadership of the Party. The fear was continually expressed that Deng's reforms were moving China away from socialist models of the economy and opening the country to the decadence of the West.

As mentioned above, the problem lies in the two conflicting wings within the wider umbrella of China's Communist party. The "hardliners" (of whom the Gang of Four would be an example and Li Peng another) believe that correct Marxist ideology and its communication to all within the State is the key to national prosperity. It has been said of them that they "do not care whether the cat can catch mice or not, as long as it is pure red"! Thus they allowed economic – industrial and agricultural – chaos and failure for the years of the Cultural Revolution, intent only of pursuing a course of destroying all that was "anti-patriotic" or "counter-revolutionary" – to be defined as anyone or anything they regarded as incorrect in terms of their narrow and personal view of Marxism. Thus for them economic chaos and industrial failure were an acceptable price to pay for the pursuit of ideological purity. This is the thinking of the leaders who held on to power through the Tiananmen massacre.

On the other hand, the "moderates" or "reformers" hold a different philosophy which is much more economically pragmatic. It can be summed up by the catchphrase "as long as the cat can catch mice, it does not matter what shade of red it is". They saw that economic advancement had to come to China and that it had to come quickly. China had to open up to the West, in whatever way was necessary to get Western technology, investment and help.

Christians in China have benefitted from this more pragmatic or moderate approach to Marxist ideology. They have been released from prison to take part in the Four Modernisations programme. Apart from the fact that they are needed to help in the programme, it is necessary for China also to present the illusion of religious freedom to the West. China realised – or did until June 1979 – how much the human rights issue affects trade and diplomatic relations, and will do just enough on this issue to ensure that the West is placated.

However there was one critical factor that was not fully appreciated in the early years of the Four Modernisations programme, with the apparent massive changes that swept over China. It was all too easy to see the changes in China and imagine that the openness to the West meant that the government was moving away from its strict adherence to Communist principles. Deng Xiaoping, the little "emperor", the architect of the new policies, was more complex than he had at first seemed. The key lay in his fiercely cherished view that economic change was essential and imperative; but political change was unnecessary and to be resisted at all costs. He had seemed to be "liberal" in Marxist political terms – but he was not. Hence his willingness to slaughter students in central Beijing and his several times repeated statement that the shedding of blood was totally acceptable to maintain hardline political orthodoxy and the supremacy of his cherished Four Principles.

Many, including myself in the early days, did not understand the man and his complexity – and political savagery. Because of that, he will forfeit his chance to go down as a significant leader in China's history. Rather he is likely to be seen as one of a long line of emperors for whom, at the end of the day, the people's lives were highly expendable commodities.

In 1986, before any of these most recent events had hit the international consciousness, Deng said this: "Without leadership by the Communist Party and without socialism, there is no future for China. This truth has been demonstrated in the past, and it will be demonstrated again in the future...We cannot do without dictatorship. We must not only affirm the need for it, but exercise it when necessary. Of course, we must be cautious about resorting to dictatorial means and make as few arrests as possible."

A major turning point in the reforms programme seemed to come at the 13th Congress of the Chinese Communist Party, held in October 1987. Deng retired from all but one of his posts, thus putting pressure on the other older leaders to do the same. Among these would have been most of the old men who objected to the reforms programme. This clever strategy on the part of Deng allowed younger men into positions of power who would be more likely to carry on with the programme of reforms. However, in the face of that apparent victory for the moderates, the end of 1987 and beginning of 1988 saw a swing back to a tougher approach. A more austere season began, leading to the slaughter of the students and others and the hardline crackdown and purges of 1989.

China at the end of the 20th Century

The contrast with the Soviets at this point is highly significant. The post-1976 third period in China saw the attempt to bring economic change with no political change of any kind — hence the student demands for democracy. They knew that the economic policies had led to a situation where they would no longer see much more advancement without decentralisation and a loosening of party control and corruption. Deng was not willing to do that. The Soviets under Gorbachev have approached the matter from precisely the opposite place, going first — on the surface at least — for major change in the political sphere under the glasnost policies and holding back much more on the economic side. It is a vital drama that is being played out before our eyes by the two Marxist superpowers.

Which way will China — or Russia — go? We do not know. Certainly the hardliners on both sides are always regrouping, ready to pounce back if economic policies falter, as in China in 1988 where the nation had nearly 40 percent inflation. The hardliners in both nations point to the corruption that increased openness brings and to social unrest — amongst the minority populations in both nations and among intellectuals and dissenters. The red cat waits to pounce once more, keen to impose its total ideological orthodoxy. What a challenge to prayer for believing Christians is presented by both China and Russia today.

In China, we have seen many swings and counter-swings between the "hardliners" and the "liberals" over the last few years. In 1983 and 1987 there were conservative crackdowns on some of the 'liberal' ideas. Tighter control was once more exercised for some time, but nowhere near as strict as under the Cultural Revolution. Western observers, however, were concerned that China's open policy might be affected and any progress that had been made brought to a standstill. The events of 1989 have involved another swing towards the hardliners. We cannot say how long this will last. International isolation will not serve China's economic aspirations.

In order to assess the future, we must learn from recent events. The Party is committed to retaining its grip on power, even if that grip becomes a little less obvious at times — and a little more obvious at others. The State still exercises a great deal of control over the lives of individuals and institutions, including the church.

For the future, we must wait — and pray. When I was in China in 1980 during the trial of the Gang of Four, Chinese television carried the trial nightly. At one point most of the staff in the hotel where I was staying seemed to disappear — only to be discovered crammed into the TV room watching reports of the Gang of Four being tried. No Superbowl, no Cup Final ever held more rapt attention for people than these events did for them. But it is not these events that remain with me so much as a statement by a godly Christian. "God has answered our prayers", he proclaimed. It was not Mao, or Deng or the Gang of Four or any others who had written the scripts and ultimately directed the affairs of men and women in China. It is a loving God in response to a praying and believing people.

The message and proclamation of this praying Christian needs to be heard by the Christian church worldwide. To that church his words are more than a testimony about the past. They are a challenge for the future, as we see China's glories and its shames paraded before us by our media. If God has answered prayer on that scale already for the greatest nation upon earth, the nation of China, can and will He not do it again?

But what of the church in China today? Into what shapes and forms has it been moulded by China's troubled past? How is it facing up to an uncertain future? We shall begin to consider these questions in the following two chapters.

CHAPTER 4

THE THREE SELF
PATRIOTIC MOVEMENT

The Three Self Patriotic Movement (TSPM) is the organisation established by the Party and the government in China to liaise between the government and the Protestant churches. As such it is not a church, but it is the officially recognised instrument of leadership of China's Protestant church. The Party also sees the TSPM as 'the voice' of the Protestant church in China. Of course many Christians in China, as we shall see, do not accept that. But that is the view of the authorities. It is impossible to understand the situation in China unless we have some understanding of the TSPM.

1. The Origins and History of the TSPM.

i) Pre-Revolutionary China and the 1950's.
In the 19th century, a Presbyterian missionary by the name of John Nevius put forward the suggestion that the Asian church should be self-governing (in administration), self-supporting (in finance), and self-propagating (in evangelisation). I do not know

whether the idea originated with Nevius. But I do know that it is that 'Three Self' thinking that is the basis of what is now called the Three Self Patriotic Movement in China.

The concept was taken up by many of the churches in Nevius' time, and by the time of the Communist victory in 1949 there were some genuine and successful attempts from various quarters — missionary and Chinese — to produce truly indigenous churches, incorporating the policy set out by John Nevius into church life.

Against that background, in September 1949, a certain Wu Yaotsung led a Protestant delegation in the first "Chinese People's Political Consultative Conference' in Beijing. Wu was not seen as representative by many of China's Christians. His own basis of faith — or lack of it — appeared at times to be more derived from socialist than Biblical doctrine. He seemed to have considerable doubts about the resurrection of the Lord Jesus from the dead, and about miracles in general. More seriously, he and those around him did not seem to feel that their denial of fundamental Biblical truths was of any significance in their supposed and self-claimed leadership of the Chinese church. China's largely evangelical church was not quick to accept leadership from such a source — it bore the marks of a political, rather than a spiritual, agenda.

A year later, Wu and twenty other Protestant leaders met with Zhou Enlai to produce a draft document that was entitled the 'Christian Manifesto'. This document was basically a statement of loyalty by the church in China to the Chinese Communist Party.

Among those things designated as the church's responsibility in Chinese society were the following: Christian churches and organisations should give complete support to the 'Common Political Platform' and under the leadership of the government, oppose imperialism, feudalism, and bureaucratic capitalism. They should take part in the effort to build an independent, democratic, peaceable, unified, prosperous and powerful China.

They should also do their utmost to ensure that people in churches everywhere recognise clearly the evils that had been wrought in China by imperialism. They should take effective measures to cultivate a patriotic and democratic spirit among their adherents, as well as a psychology of self-respect and self-reliance.

The Manifesto was officially published in September 1950 and signed by 400,000 Christians.

In 1951 over 150 leaders attended a national conference in Beijing, which was to deal with 'the disposal of the properties of American-subsidised missionary groups in China'. One result of the conference was the establishing of the 'Oppose America, Aid (North) Korea, Three Self Reform Movement of the Church of Christ in China' or 'Three Self Reform Church'. An official slogan was adopted: 'Love Country. Love Church', and Wu Yaotsung was elected leader. The present day Three Self Patriotic Church is directly and inseparably linked to that beginning.

At the same time all Christians were expected to give their consent to the 'Christian Manifesto'. Notable among those who refused to do so were men like Watchman Nee and Wang Mingdao. They were not in agreement with the Party's attempt to gain control over all the churches in China. They certainly wanted nothing to do with a movement that would be subject to Party policy.

In this lies part of the heart of the matter. A number of believers were then and have since been accused of being "anti-patriotic" or "anti-revolutionary". That is not true. They love China, and are not politically active against the government. Their opposition is to elements within the TSPM, and its highly political agenda. It is a statement of great content, then, if opposition to the TSPM is seen as being "anti-patriotic", for it puts the TSPM into a political, not a spiritual, category.

In 1954 the National Christian Council held its first meeting. At this gathering the emphasis shifted from 'reform' to 'patriotism'. The 'Three Self Patriotic Movement' (TSPM) was established, with Wu Yaotsung as its chairman. The movement was responsible to the Religious Affairs Bureau, which is part of the government's United Front Work Department.

By 1955, pastors and church workers who had refused to affiliate themselves with the TSPM came under vicious attack. Wang Mingdao, who had been born in 1900 during the Boxer rebellion, was a man with whom the Communists found it very difficult to find fault in terms of his spiritual walk or Christian service. He was pastor of an indigenous work in Beijing. He was, however, charged with being anti-government and anti-Three Self. He was accused by the TSPM of being 'head of the counter-revolutionary foreign infiltration' and as a result spent a total of twenty-three years in prison — from 1955 until 1978. In the initial phase of his imprisonment he was subjected to over a year of mental torture.

As I write this, Wang Mingdao still lives, and although he is very deaf and virtually blind, and his wife is also nearly blind, they are both very alert and well-informed about what is happening concerning the church in China. He still speaks out strongly against the TSPM, an organisation he says was founded by an atheist (Wu Yaotsung).

The experiences of Wang Mingdao and his wife were mirrored in countless other lives, though the sacrifices of that multitude will only be revealed in eternity. Some leaders, pastors and others in the TSPM played their part in the imprisonment of many of these faithful servants of God, actively denouncing these evangelical brethren, or simply maintaining an evil silence and refusing to come to their defence.

In 1957 a further purge took place, this time labelled the 'Anti-rightist' campaign. During this further hostile period, Christians who were opposed to the TSPM were branded as 'rightist' and suffered accordingly.

By 1958 the TSPM had put out a decree forbidding all private house meetings. At a TSPM conference held in Jiangsu it was decided that 'all so called churches, worship halls and family meetings which have been established without the permission of the government must be dissolved'.

In Shanghai, the TSPM churches resolved 'not to invite freelance evangelists to preach in our churches, and not to attend or preach in underground services in homes'. In the same city, the number of churches had been reduced from two hundred to under twenty. In Beijing, the number had been reduced to four from an original sixty-six places of worship. The pastors from these churches were sent to the countryside for re-education.

In many cities only one Protestant church was allowed to remain open. The leaders of these few remaining churches were undoubtedly those who were prepared to compromise with the Communist Party. Through the TSPM, the Party gave strict instructions about the sort of topic on which the leaders could preach. Anything considered counter to the aims of the Party was forbidden.

It would appear that many Christians stopped attending the small number of churches that were left open, because they were TSPM controlled and had frequently become centres for political indoctrination, rather than for preaching the gospel.

During this period of the late 1950's China saw the first signs of what has come to be known as the House Church movement. We shall have more to say about that in the next chapter. For the present it is enough to say that some Chinese Christians felt that the only choice before them lay between the highly political and compromised TSPM or no worship at all. They therefore sought for another choice — and began to meet in great secrecy in their homes. That was natural to a society which has traditionally placed great emphasis on the family.

There was great danger for them in doing this and the authorities arrested believers for exercising that right. There is no doubt that some of the TSPM leadership were involved in the betrayal to the authorities and therefore, the subsequent arrest of Christians who were meeting in this way. We need to know that, if we are to understand why some believers in China, especially perhaps those who know what happened during that period of the late 1950's, feel that they are unable to trust or work with the TSPM to this very day.

ii) The Cultural Revolution.

In 1966 the Cultural Revolution exploded on to the scene. That ushered in a new period of great violence for the church. Nor was it just the independent house churches that suffered. All churches were closed, including those controlled by the TSPM. For one period of time there was no freedom of religion whatsoever. Most pastors were arrested, imprisoned, even killed. Much Christian literature was burnt or systematically hunted out and destroyed. I have heard of one old saint who only kept her Bible by burying it in the earth of a flower-pot. Many Christians suffered during the Cultural Revolution. But by God's mercy the embattled house churches not only survived — they grew!

The Cultural Revolution finally ended in 1976, yet in its wake there remained a legacy. The TSPM was still regarded with great caution by many, especially those who had suffered. They were suspicious of pastors who had preached in the TSPM churches, but who had denied their faith and even betrayed their fellow Christians during the accusation campaigns. Again, we may take the case of Wang Mingdao. Both his church and the magazine that he published were registered with the government. Yet the TSPM had endorsed the twenty-three year prison sentence imposed upon him.

iii) 1976 — the present day.

After 1976, with the death of Mao and the rise of Deng, the United Front Work Department was reinstated and, under it, the Religious Affairs Bureau (RAB) was restored. It was established that five recognised religions, including Roman Catholicism (the Catholic Patriotic Association) and the Protestant TSPM would, under the watchful eye of the RAB, take on the responsibility of implementing the government's religious policy.

Churches had already begun to be reopened under the auspices of the TSPM as early as 1979. There was a concerted effort made to draw people back to them and the authorities even went so far as to try and persuade genuine evangelical pastors to return to TSPM pulpits, sometimes from the labour camps. In fact, many believers flooded back to some of the newly opened TSPM churches, rejoicing that once more they could worship openly and relatively freely in China's cities. It is said that the authorities were amazed when some of the Shanghai churches saw lines of people coming very early in the morning to get a seat when the churches opened in 1979. I believe that many of these folk simply rejoiced that they could again express their love of the Lord Jesus legally, together with their fellow believers.

It was then decided, in October 1980, to form a new organisation, called the China Christian Council (CCC). This new body would concentrate on the religious affairs of the church, while the TSPM would look after the political side. Bishop Ding was elected president of the CCC and chairman of the TSPM. The function of the TSPM was henceforth to make sure that all religious affairs were 'legitimate activities'.

The government's policy on religion was issued in March 1982 to all Party workers in Document 19 of the Chinese Communist Party's Central Committee. It is important to understand that Document 19 was not meant to be seen or read by most people. It was intended to be an in-house document for party members only. It is therefore very significant that we have been able to see it, leaked as it was to sources in Hong Kong. It does represent the official party line, even during that relatively benign period. It is the hard face of Chinese Communist reality, behind the mask of claimed religious liberty, telling us what really is and is not allowed.

Although statements like Document 19 permitted a limited amount of religious freedom, many activities were forbidden for China's Christians, TSPM and house church alike: Sunday schools, all evangelism among people under the age of 18 years, evangelism outside of church buildings registered with the TSPM, and all 'feudal superstitions', among which could be counted casting out demons and praying for healing. The official policy towards the house churches was made clear. They were not to be tolerated; but they should not be stamped out too quickly, because of their deep roots amongst the people. It is at least encouraging that the Christian house churches came in for mention in such a document, for it shows the reality of their presence in China.

By 1982 the TSPM had established itself firmly at the provincial level. Steps were then taken to increase control further by establishing the supervision of Christians at county level. The attempts to set up TSPM and CCC organisations at this level were sometimes resisted, however, in areas where the house churches were strongest.

Some Christians in Dongyang County, in Zhejiang province, sent a letter to all Christians throughout the county requesting prayer. The TSPM had tried to set itself up there, but most of the Christians in the area opposed this and prayed and fasted for three days. The letter claimed that TSPM officials had stirred up the local militia to attack a meeting place and physically assault believers. This kind of behaviour points to the more militant "hardline" element within the TSPM,

60

which clearly exists on a national and local level. Substantial evidence points to their often brutal cooperation against believers with local security forces, in their attempts to stamp out any person or practice of which they do not approve. It is important to see that implementation of TSPM policies may differ widely in different places and areas of China, depending on the nature of the local TSPM leadership — whether it is "hardline" or "moderate".

By 1989 over 5,000 churches are said to have been reopened under the auspices of the TSPM. In many of them there is good preaching, Bible studies and prayer meetings. There are many genuine Christians who attend TSPM churches, who have no idea of the political or spiritual implications of their belonging to such a church. There are also a good number of sound, Bible believing pastors. The issue lies with the top leadership of the TSPM, which is strongly influenced by loyalty to the Party. In the leadership of a TSPM church on a local level, normally one of the leaders will be politically orientated, responsible for seeing that Party policy is adhered to and the rules kept.

2. An evangelical perpective on the TSPM

i) A general assessment.

If the organisation of the TSPM is viewed as a pyramid, the top (or pointed) part of the structure, the smallest but most visible part, contains the political element, or the Party members who exercise control. Underneath them are the pastors, largely evangelical and desiring to serve God and His people. At the bottom of the pyramid, the widest and largest portion, are the laity, the general evangelical strata of the church.

In 1988 a copy of a letter reached the West, written by an elderly pastor who had suffered greatly during the Cultural Revolution and had been imprisoned for many years. After his release he served the Lord in the house churches, but when the TSPM set up a church in his city, he was invited to preach in it. He accepted the invitation because he saw the needs of the people. So while sympathising with the house churches, he now regularly preaches in the TSPM church. This man, who is not extreme in his views, has provided very interesting information for us in his letter about the top leadership of the TSPM.

He claims that the leadership of the TSPM at national, provincial and municipal levels are, for the most part, either underground Party workers or former church workers who after 1956 entered the Party.

He also claims that Bishop Ding Guangxun, current leader of the TSPM, joined the Party in the forties when a student at St. John's University Theological Seminary. Apparently, the old pastor was told by a relatively high provincial official of the RAB: "Ding Guangxun is the Secretary of the Party Committee within Protestantism and is also Secretary for the overall Party committee controlling the major religions at the national level. Ding is a veteran Party member. In the Party his position is higher than that of the Section Heads of the RAB or even the Head of the RAB." Other evidence would point to the possibility of these statements being accurate. What makes them serious is that Bishop Ding heads up the TSPM, the CCC and the main TSPM seminary in Nanjing.

A recent study of the top provincial leadership of the TSPM and CCC shows that the hard line political old guard still control the movement. Some of the leaders are known to be former persecutors of the church.

While evangelicals within the TSPM seem to have a certain amount of freedom in some areas of the country, overall the organisation is controlled by Party members. The founding 'vision' of the TSPM openly states that the aim of the organisation is to 'rally all Christians under the leadership of the Chinese Communist Party and the People's Government'.

With a nation as large as China, different regions will sustain different views of the TSPM. There is a fairly wide spectrum of opinion among house church Christians about the organisation. Some are totally firm in their opposition to it; others are prepared to co-operate to some degree, and others yet register their meetings as government approved 'meeting points'.

ii) Some of the issues.

The arguments for and against involvement with the TSPM are many. Pastors who are against co-operation would argue along the following lines:

. . . "Christ or Caesar". Christ is the Lord of the Church and is, therefore, the only One who has final authority on matters that relate to the Church. In TSPM churches the Communist Party has the final say on many issues which are the sole concern of those churches. Their motto is 'Aiguo, Aijiau' — 'Love Your Country, Love Your Religion' in that order. If Christ is not the head of the body, argue these pastors, is the body beneath really the genuine church?

. . . The TSPM appears to be supporting and establishing the church, but in fact sometimes has acted and does act in ways that are in opposition to this. It has at times restricted as much as possible the development of the church, yet has put on a public face of righteousness.

. . . The government will make use of the TSPM to infiltrate and take control of the house churches. This has been experienced. In one particularly well known house church, the TSPM offered help in the form of Bibles, hymnbooks and preachers. But the price could well have been that the leadership of the house church would have been effectively replaced by TSPM-approved personnel. Others point to the fact that lists of names gathered by the TSPM in the 50's formed one basis for government attacks on Christians.

Leaders who feel that a degree of co-operation is

possible, would argue that:

. . . There are many people whose only chance ever to hear the gospel is in a TSPM church, especially those who live in the cities. The TSPM should not be blindly opposed merely for the sake of it. At least there are many godly TSPM pastors, and those that are not would not at present be audacious enough publicly to oppose Christ in the pulpit.

. . . The TSPM at least provides legitimacy from the state to Christianity as a framework within which the church can grow. The trellis (TSPM) may be dead, but the vine has life.

The main point of contention, as far as most leaders are concerned, is to do with the principle of the spiritual independence of the church. While many recognise that there are godly men serving as pastors in TSPM churches, they are very doubtful about the motives of the top leadership and the ultimate aims of the Party — and indeed of that top leadership — towards the house churches.

iii) Some examples of meetings and documents.
EXAMPLE 1: In August 1987, the Standing Committee of the national TSPM met for an important conference in Chengdu. A report from a reliable source throws some light on the question of what exactly the TSPM is attempting to do in the church.

Baptism: Those under 18 years of age are not allowed to be baptised. Any applications for baptism have to be investigated and approved by the TSPM, the Religious Affairs Bureau and other relevant departments.

Qualifications for leaders: Pastors must have definite theological training, and helpers must have gone through definite Three Self training. They must 'love country and love religion', be law abiding, and be able to lead believers along the Three Self road. Leaders who repeatedly disobey the system can be dismissed from the ministry and even be erased from the church register.

Those who act illegally should be reported to the government to be dealt with in accordance with the law. (It should be noted that "illegal" means meetings and evangelism not approved by the TSPM).

Leaders must be approved by the county, city and provincial RAB, United Front Work Department and TSPM. These leaders must pass examination and political investigation, and only then apply to be preachers. 'Self appointed evangelists' who do not have a letter of introduction from the province or city organisations must be prohibited and reported to the higher authorities. Meeting points must get approval and carry out the 'Three Designates' — that is 1. Designate the staff. 2. Designate the meeting place. (This has not been universally applied). 3. Designate the parish. Later a 4th designate has sometimes been added — designate the time.

Financial Matters: Contributions from abroad must be dealt with according to national TSPM regulations. Ten percent of believers contributions in every church and meeting point have to be given to provincial and city TSPM organisations for office expenses.

EXAMPLE 2: A further example of the type of information given out by TSPM leaders was a statement made by Bishop Ding in September 1987. In it he stated that no Christian churches had to register with the authorities in any form. This statement was given a great deal of publicity in the West. Yet it can be shown from the TSPM's own internal documentation that all churches and house churches have to register with the relevant Party and State authorities, or be prepared to suffer the inevitable consequences if their 'illegal' activities are discovered.

In fact, shortly after Bishop Ding's statement, new regulations to this effect were issued in one of China's most economically advanced provinces, Guangdong, right on Hong Kong's doorstep. Among other things, these regulations stated:

— All places for religious worship (including Christian meeting points or house churches) must register with the Religious Affairs Bureau or be closed down.

— No-one except registered Christian workers can evangelise or preach.

— All religious literature must obtain approval for publication from the Religious Affairs Bureau (which as a Party organ is staffed by atheists).

— Those who disobey these regulations will be 'criticised and re-educated' by the Religious Affairs Bureau, or in serious cases dealt with by the Public Security Bureau.

Though subsequently Bishop Ding has opposed these regulations, taking in fact a clear stand against them, past history shows a reluctance by many outside of China to face up to that evident source of pressure by the TSPM, or certain wings of it, upon China's ordinary believers.

It is hardly surprising that many Christians who are basically hard working, loyal members of society find such regulations too much to accept and consequently leave the TSPM churches to worship and serve God in the house churches. It is estimated that in a small area of one province alone nearly 50,000 people left TSPM churches in one year.

I have heard of one 'non-registered' (itinerant) evangelist who has been on the road for five years, preaching from village to village. He has hardly been able to see his family during that time. If he returns home he would almost certainly be arrested because he is regarded as an illegal evangelist. We have honestly to face TSPM complicity in such policies. In effect, that leads them to oppose those who risk their all to spread the Gospel. The situation may become yet more difficult for those who seek to preach the Gospel in that way in China in obedience to the Lord's clear command. Firstly, the Li Peng government, as long as it remains in power, it likely to take a tough line against that kind of activity. Secondly, the introduction of identity cards in China will make it harder to travel in order to preach the Gospel. We need to pray for such men and women.

EXAMPLE 3. In another leaked secret document, probably dating from a period of great freedom under the sponsorship of Hu Yaobang around 1985, totally unexpected confirmation of the methods employed by the TSPM came from a possible senior Party leader. Under the pen name Ru Wen, this individual pointed out that the repressive policies being implemented were of little use in stopping the growth of the church. He even stated that there were certain TSPM leaders who 'did not love their religion', who could not be counted as representative of the Christians in China, and who were actually alienating believers from the Party.

The TSPM authorities also object very strongly to the help that is given to the house churches by organisations outside the country. Much needed material is channelled into China through Hong Kong. Almost daily, materials pour in — Bibles, reference books, teaching tapes as well as the radio programmes that reach deep into China's heartland.

Such activity is attacked by the TSPM in no uncertain terms, and is regarded as foreign interference. They constantly state that there is no need for Bibles or Christian literature to be supplied from outside of China, yet we know from experience that there is a Bible famine among believers. Some are prepared to travel hundreds of miles at the mere possibility of being able to get hold of Bibles.

The TSPM does produce Bibles on its own printing press (the Amity Press), supplied by Bible Societies in the West, but the quantity produced is still very small compared to the great need. In addition, some believers fear that, if they want a Bible from the TSPM, they may have to register and fill out very detailed forms. Whether this is true or not on an ongoing basis needs to be confirmed. The Amity Printing Press has produced Bibles of various kinds and plans to do more. That is good, and we should be grateful for that initiative. A new simplified character cross-reference Bible, ethnic (Korean etc) Bibles are all to be highly welcomed and applauded. But it would be a tragedy if the presence of such a facility in Nanjing led us to believe that it could meet the needs of China's Christian population. It is a significant, but only very partial, answer to that problem.

The CCC and the TSPM have always emphasised the need to purge the country of 'imperialist elements' and to make Christianity a totally Chinese religion. They want no help, or what they would regard as interference, from outside of China. In January 1988 a new policy statement was issued by the United Front Work Department:

'Believers and non-believers must be united and their will and strength concentrated on building socialism with Chinese characteristics. Thus in foreign exchanges in the religious sphere we must uphold the 'Three Self' principles for running the church, and not allow any foreign forces to control our religious bodies or religious affairs'.

The great majority of the house churches, however, while emphasising the basic principles of self reliance, believe it is biblical to maintain fellowship with and receive support from Christians outside China. They would however totally agree that the Chinese church should in no way be dominated or controlled by any outside forces — whether they be the Chinese government or foreign influences.

3. Two recent puzzles.

As I write, two events have occurred recently that further confuse a difficult picture.

Puzzle 1. There is a possibility that the TSPM could be replaced by another organisation in the not too distant future. Bishop Ding, at the beginning of 1989, clearly stated in an interview to News Network International that the TSPM would be dissolved by 1991, and that he himself would stand down. Two months later a statement was issued claiming that no such decision had been made, and that the matter was under discussion only.

I personally believe that there is a power struggle going on between the 'hardliners' and the 'moderates' within the TSPM, and that Bishop Ding at this time sits with the moderates. It is reported that, in a sermon published in the 'Jinling Theological Review', Bishop Ding stated that he had followed the "leftist" line in the past. Now he wanted to devoted his energies to fight leftism. He is reported to have said that "On certain questions, I adhered to this line". In order to show penitence "I throw myself into the work of opposing leftism. Now, whether in the seminary, in the church or in society, I devote all my energy to not allowing leftist things to continue to harm people; may God accept this my sign of repentance. In politics, leftism attacks good people and reduces the scope of unity, while from the point of view of faith, leftism tramples love underfoot and denies the Gospel. In opposing leftism today, we lift up love, spreading the spirit of mutual love in this world, and causing love, Christ's love, to revive many cold hearts." (CNCR 1380. June 16th, 1989).

I believe that that statement lies behind some changes in posture by Bishop Ding. It is, however, likely that official statements from the TSPM under the Li Peng government will restore leftist positions, whatever the heart feelings of TSPM leaders like Ding might be. They cannot speak openly like that in the present season and remain in office.

It also raises another interesting question. If Bishop Ding is confessing that his (and therefore the TSPM's) leadership has been tainted by leftism which "attacks good people", what is the position now of liberal church leaders outside of China who have held doggedly to Ding's authority over the last decade. They have solidly denied this harm caused by leftist elements in the TSPM, especially to the house churches in China. They have held up Bishop Ding, who is now confessing past errors, as the rightful head of all Christians in China. Could they perhaps admit their errors as well?

But it is early days yet, and we shall have to await events. The lessons of history would suggest that Christians outside China should learn not to be naive and overly accepting of such statements. Often we do not understand what is going on behind the scenes.

Puzzle 2. All of that has further been complicated by Bishop Ding's open and very brave statement in favour of the Tiananmen students in late May of 1989. The statement urged the government to negotiate with the students, and expressed solidarity with their cause. That means, with the June massacre (which Ding in his public statement expressly urged the government not to undertake), that a significant and dangerous shadow has fallen across the life of the church in China.

Up to this point, the TSPM has been careful never to disagree with the State. The line has hitherto been drawn between TSPM and the Party on the one side, and those regarded as the enemies at any given time on the other side — Wang Mingdao in the 50's, the house churches in Canton or elsewhere in the 80's. Now there is a danger, if Bishop Ding's statement is held to be representative of the Chinese church in general and is called unpatriotic, of the line being drawn between the state on the one side, and the church — TSPM and house church alike — on the other.

These are complex and difficult days for the church in China. They demand much prayer and concern for TSPM and house churches alike. We do not yet know what will happen. But we do know that the church of Jesus Christ was born at a difficult time, under Roman occupation, with much stacked against it. From that small beginning it has grown and flourished and multiplied. We know too that the same Lord Jesus Who reigned then reigns now, and that He knows the way to go. China's church and Christians have surely more — much more — with which to thrill us in the days to come!

4. Some conclusions.

It is, then, very difficult for believers on the outside fully to grasp the situation, and to make sense out of the apparently conflicting reports that reach them. Here are some suggested guidelines:

i) *Remember that you only hear one voice (the TSPM's), unless you have the kind of sources inside and outside of China available to very few of us.*
The TSPM leadership, especially when travelling abroad, lays great emphasis on the fact that there is complete unity in the church in China. House church leaders, on the other hand, often completely deny any such unity with the TSPM. The TSPM claims to be the true voice for the church in China, a church which it claims numbers around 5 million believers and 5,000 churches. From many reports that reach us other than through the TSPM, however, it is estimated that the number of believers is more likely to be as many as 50 million. Can the TSPM still claim to be a voice for the majority of a church it denies even to exist?

The problem is exacerbated by the fact that the voices of the house churches are very often drowned out by the very plausible and reasonable sounding information which is released by the TSPM. This information is then transmitted uncritically to a large audience outside China. Hence my heartcry from the Chens in the first chapter — and the need for many more to be broader reporters of the unheard, non-official TSPM voice of the church in China.

The result is that large sections of the church outside of China receive uncritically the TSPM line, as is the case with the British and other Councils of Churches and even large denominations. Visitors to China can be easily misled into thinking that all is well on the Christian scene in the country, when real tensions exist. How can such visitors speak with any authority when they have no firsthand experience of the persecution which is still very much a fact of life for believers in certain areas? Their information is often funnelled through very narrow TSPM sources, and they have no access to house church sources.

Whatever one may feel about the TSPM, many observers of the Chinese Christian scene would agree on one thing — it is not the only or even the true voice of the church in China. Its approach has become more subtle and sophisticated since Wu Yaotsung's days, but the problems at the heart of the matter remain the same.

ii) *Remember that certain elements of the TSPM do not work for the good of the church of Jesus Christ. They work for the party. They are often the ones whose voice reaches you. They are utterly unrepresentative of China's Christians.*

The TSPM has initiated a campaign deliberately intended to confuse and divide evangelical opinion in the West about the church in China. In November 1987, the official TSPM magazine openly boasted of TSPM success in wooing major evangelical denominations and seminaries into supporting it, announcing that it had "lit a fire in the evangelicals' own back yard".

Behind the smokescreen of disinformation, conflicting reports and even lies, the relentless campaign to limit the work of the gospel continues. The true church of Christ, in TSPM and house churches alike, suffers as vigorous attempts are made to bring all its activities under state control.

Today the TSPM uses evangelical language and has a definite and consistent policy. It divides people into 3 categories — enemies, uncertain middle territory to be influenced and finally friends. The friends are those who acknowledge that TSPM is the rightful leader of all the churches in China. The middle group are those who can be influenced, and the main target is the evangelicals.

iii) *Remember to be consistent in our evangelical approach.* When all the pros and cons are weighed up, however, the real question about acknowledging who represents the church in China comes down to this: would Christians in your country ask a man to be leader of their church if that man says that God does not mind if millions of Chinese do not believe in Him; who has no clear personal testimony, or burden for the millions of unconverted people in his land. Such a man, from his public statements, is Bishop Ding. If we would not accept such a man for our own churches, why do we accept the TSPM leadership as the rightful and only voice of the church in China?

CHAPTER 5

CHINA'S HOUSE CHURCHES

In China the term "house church" signifies a group of Christian believers, sometimes numbering several hundred, who meet in a home or a farmhouse or some other informal building (or even sometimes in the open air). The first thing, then, we may safely say about the house churches is that they do not always meet in houses! They meet for prayer, Bible study, ministry and mutual encouragement. They may meet this way for a variety of reasons. One reason may be geographical considerations — it is often the only way they can meet, for there often are no official churches in their area. Another reason may be spiritual conviction — even where there are official churches, they wish to have real fellowship and proper instruction in the word of God. Yet another reason may be fear. They simply do not dare to be seen worshipping openly. This is particularly so of small home groups. One way or the other, it is often a question of sheer practical necessity.

Whereas home meetings are still a fairly new phenomenon in the West, they are nothing new for many Chinese Christians, especially those who live in the rural areas. Even before the Communist victory in 1949, such meetings were not uncommon. But the period of 40 years since 1949 has proved to be the furnace out of which this remarkable phenomenon of the Twentieth Century church has been forged. Later in the book I shall draw some spiritual lessons from these churches. In this chapter my aim is simply to make sure that we have a clear picture of what we mean by this evocative term "house churches".

1. The history of the house churches in China.

For the sake of clarity I would like to divide the history of China's house church movement into three periods, as I did with the history of the TSPM. That must in part be a random division, of course. The three periods are the late 50's; the period of the Cultural Revolution; and the post 1978 period.

Period 1 — the Late 50's

I have already touched on this period in the last chapter, but let me do so again. In the fifties, as pressure from the Communists began to increase, and the TSPM began to demand an essentially political allegiance from all Christians, many of those who refused to conform began quietly to meet in homes. In the countryside, where many of the churches had been closed down, house meetings became the only way for believers to gather for worship, teaching and fellowship. In the cities too, as Party policy began to bite and the majority of churches were also closed, many Christians began to meet clandestinely, often in as small numbers as two or three people. They gathered to pray, to encourage each other and to break bread.

To meet in such a way was not strange for Chinese people. Chinese culture had always laid great emphasis on family life, and even though Communism has done much to try and destroy this, it has largely failed. It was then natural for Christians to centre their spiritual lives in the home. Their house meetings were but an extension of their everyday lives. It would also prove to be the salvation of the church in China, but even more excitingly, the seedbeds out of which would come growth on an explosive scale.

The government was soon made aware of the widespread nature of home meetings and took active steps to suppress them. By 1958, in both the cities and the countryside, virtually all churches had been closed. The problem of Christians meeting in homes was far greater for the authorities in the countryside, however, because they were often remote and less easily controlled. Yet the State still pursued a relentless policy whereby private meetings — that is those not held in TSPM churches — were forbidden. If more than two people were found praying together, they would be liable to be prosecuted on charges of counter-revolutionary activity and sent to prison.

For a number of years many Christians met secretly in this way, risking arrest, prosecution, persecution and imprisonment. Adherence to the Scriptures, communal prayer and worship was only possible outside of the State controlled churches in this period.

I have already made it clear that the origins of much house church distrust of the TSPM lies in this period of the 1950's. The active participation in the arrests of some of those early house church members by TSPM members — some of whom still are leaders in the TSPM today — has left deep scars. It is not to be seen, at least in some cases, as a lack of forgiveness by the house church leaders towards these TSPM leaders, nor is there any basic desire not to see them restored. They simply cannot accept that an apparent total lack of repentance for betrayal of their brethren is consistent with spiritual leadership of the church in China.

Period 2 — The Cultural Revolution.
With the outbreak of the Cultural Revolution in 1966

came the fresh onslaught on the church of Jesus Christ. Even the few remaining TSPM churches were closed, and institutional Christianity was completely eradicated from the life of China. As we have noted before, Bibles were burnt, and many pastors and believers were sent to prison or labour camps. House meetings continued, however, even though they had become even more dangerous than ever before.

In one province, during this extremely difficult time, meetings of people in groups of three or four would take place at night, for prayer and Scripture reading. In spite of all the restrictions, personal witness continued. As well as gathering in homes, they would also meet in parks, under trees, where they would pray with their eyes open in order not to attract unnecessary attention. They dared not preach or sing.

In another area, a mining community, even after the Red Guards had arrived and confiscated all the Bibles and Christian literature they could find, a group of about one hundred people continued to meet in one of the miner's dormitories for about four years. In order to avoid problems with the Red Guard Revolutionary Committee, they would sing as quietly as possible and also include a short time during each meeting for a study of the Thoughts Of Chairman Mao. Large meetings such as these were the exception, however. The majority were very small, especially in the cities where the authorities were much more able to keep things under control and surveillance was much tighter.

One report speaks of meetings of a very exceptional nature. The situation was so tight and dangerous that the meetings had to take place at a different time and a different place every week. It was too dangerous to do otherwise, for they would be quickly known and raided, and the believers arrested. But there was another problem. Given the atmosphere of supervision by others and betrayal by infiltration, it was too dangerous even to announce the meetings. The only way in which a believer could get to a meeting was to pray and ask the Lord when and where the meeting was to take place. I cannot help wondering how we would fare under those circumstances!

The house churches in China were born, therefore, out of practical necessity springing from persecution. Especially during the Cultural Revolution, Christians had nowhere else to go. Many denominational differences that might have existed before the Communist purges were soon forgotten in the common and overriding desire to have fellowship with other believers.

Many of the groups that met were without their pastors or leaders, for many of them had been imprisoned. Yet they survived as they discovered new depths of fellowship with their fellow believers. A unity was created that many of them had not known before the outbreak of persecution and, as a result, they discovered some of the true meaning of New Testament Christianity. Buildings, regular places of worship, no longer held any importance for them as they found the truths of Scripture to be so appropriate for their situation. The Body of Christ became more important than any building, as they discovered the presence of the Holy Spirit whenever two or three gathered together in the Name of Jesus.

During this time of severe trial and testing, the church of Christ was purified. For us as onlookers, sitting in the comfort of our homes, this is an easy thing to say. But it is a sentiment that is echoed by many Chinese believers. The halfhearted, uncommitted and false disciples were weeded out when persecution hit the church. The Cultural Revolution was the crucible out of which developed a revived church.

Period 3: Post-1978 China.
In the mid seventies the situation eased a little and in some areas Christians were more bold in their witness. It was, however, sometimes still a very hazardous thing

to confess Christ too openly. Yet reports began to get through to the West of quite large house churches in existence. In one area of Fujian there were supposedly 200-300 young people meeting in unfurnished country buildings. From the same province came further reports of a Christian community that had developed in the late sixties and early seventies, which numbered around one thousand people. In 1974, five of its leaders were arrested and paraded through the streets as punishment, but later were released to continue their ministry.

Many Christians continued to be arrested until the death of Mao Tsetung in 1976, when the political climate became more relaxed. Once Deng Xiaoping had returned to power in 1978, and was engaged in the early period of the Four Modernisations with less evident political pressure, the house churches enjoyed a period of relative peace and were much freer to flourish.

The Four Modernisations so favoured by Deng and the 'open door' economic policy with the West indirectly helped the house churches to grow. The Communist Party revived the United Front Work Department, under which non-communist sectors of society no longer experienced the same kind of opposition and suppression as they had done when Mao and the Gang of Four had held sway. Instead they were encouraged to play their part in the modernisation of the country.

As part of the United Front policy, certain religious activities were once again allowed. The Communist Party would say that religious freedom was once again granted. There is, however, a world of difference between what we outside of China would understand by religious freedom, and the activities that were allowed under the new United Front policy.

As I have already said, the TSPM churches were allowed to open their doors again in 1979. Many of those churches became packed to capacity. This alerted the authorities to the number of Christians that still existed in China, in spite of the years of repression and 're-education'. But they were also made aware of the huge numbers of people involved in meeting in house churches, and the problems this would create for them in terms of effective control and supervision. Hence their rather clumsy efforts to bring all churches under the control of the TSPM, and make all meetings outside of the TSPM orbit illegal.

Between 1978 and 1980, most of the church leaders and workers who had been imprisoned falsely as 'rightists' since the fifties, or during the Cultural Revolution, were set free. The authorities were certainly not thrilled by the evidence of the survival of Christianity in their country, and the reports of incredible growth in many areas were a serious setback to their Marxist orthodoxy. The political atmosphere of the time was such, however, that repression of too open a kind would have damaged their wooing of the West, a target that was so essential for the economic, scientific and educational planks of their Four Modernisation structure.

These years were a peak period for the house churches when, in some cities, huge meetings were held every night. They took full advantage of a situation where the local Party workers were treading very cautiously in their interpretation of the more moderate religious policy, sometimes even turning a blind eye to house church activities. The Christians capitalised on the caution or confusion and became very bold, holding large meetings for the purposes of worship, teaching and evangelism.

In some areas of China the growth experienced by the house churches was nothing short of miraculous. In one county of Henan province, where before 1949 there were only about four thousand believers, the numbers rose to eighty thousand by 1982. In Ye county, nearly 10 percent of the population was estimated to be Christian in 1983. There were so many believers in Fancheng county that it was reportedly dubbed a "Jesus Nest" by local Party workers, one estimate putting the number of

Christians as high as one third of the 826,000 inhabitants. In another area there is a city where 60 percent of the population is Christian, and a city where the majority of people in the thirteen communes around the city, totalling 160,000 people, are now followers of Jesus Christ.

Some house church sources estimated the total number of Christians in Henan province to be anything up to 5 million people. In 1986 house church leaders in the province spoke of one independent grouping of house churches that now had 2,500 churches linked together in fellowship, centred in Henan, but covering five other provinces. These were at that time reported to be sending out evangelistic teams to neighbouring provinces — even as far as the border of Tibet.

Now we must look beyond the history of the house church movement in China, exciting though that may be. It does, after all, represent one of the great church growth stories of all time. We need to ask a further vital question — what posture should we, as Christians in the outside world, take towards the house churches in China. This is a very vital issue. Some folk, even some "China experts", claim that there is no such thing as a house church movement in China — they argue that the whole idea was dreamed up by some brethren in Hong Kong! That is repetition of classic Marxist disinformation, and we need to know the truth. Let me then list two key elements which should characterise our basic posture.

2. What are the house churches like today?

i) They are the majority church in China.

More than 80% of China's Christians worship in the house churches today. Some say that 95% of these Christians have come to Christ since 1976. Christianity has become indigenous through them as sometimes whole villages, or many in certain communes, have turned to Christ, due to the faithfulness and courage of house church Christians who have risked much to bring the gospel to the lost.

ii) They therefore represent the majority "voice" of China's church.

In spite of all the disinformation put out by the TSPM leadership, these people represent the genuine voice of the church in China. Up to fifty million believers in the house churches in China have a different heartcry for us to hear. What they say and what TSPM delegations say are totally different. The problem is, as I have already stressed, that they have no means to enable us to hear their voice.

Whereas the TSPM leadership states that China's Christians have no need for Bibles, Christian literature, or gospel radio, the leaders of the house churches say exactly the opposite. They tell of the great hunger there is for the word of God, and the very real famine there is, in terms of the availability of Bibles and Christian teaching materials. One Bible shared between one hundred believers is not uncommon. Portions of scripture are torn out of Bibles and circulated to be memorised, or handcopied. Sometimes these handwritten copies are circulated widely. It has been known for believers to memorise huge chunks of Scripture, even whole books. And there are many who are willing to travel hundreds of miles just to obtain Bibles for their churches from overseas sources. We shall deal later in this book with the opportunities and challenges that these needed ministries for China present to the church outside of China.

One young farmer, only recently saved, with little Bible knowledge, prepared a Bible teaching manual to help new believers, and it was estimated that this was used by at least 10,000 people. Is it any wonder that the house church leaders plead with their fellow Christians for more Bibles and more teaching materials?

They are experiencing such growth that they just cannot keep pace with the demand for teaching. Dare we on the outside, with our Bible and book mountains, ignore the pleas of our brothers and sisters? Will we allow ourselves to become deceived and lulled into apathy by the plausible sounding pronouncements of men whose first duty is not to Christ, but to the State? Do we believe those who appear to do everything to restrict the spread of the gospel, and the meeting of believers, or those who share their faith by their lives and testimony, often at great personal cost?

Do we even take the trouble to hear their voice? I am constantly amazed at the way Christian leaders in the West fail to understand the nature of information control in a Marxist society. Many do not seem to realise that any organisation, including the church, will only be allowed to exist provided it is firmly under State control. Its internal pronouncements and its official statements abroad will only be those that the party permits. As I have already explained, that is one of the functions of the TSPM. It may be that there are legitimate attempts within those strictures to fight for freedom for believers. Indeed, I am sure that some TSPM leaders feel that for them the only realistic course is to work within the "system" and courageously negotiate for as much freedom for the church as they can. But that does not mean that we believe all that is said from those circles.

But my point is addressed to Christians, and especially to Christian leaders, outside of China, not to Chinese church leaders. Can we not understand that the voices we are really needing to hear are masked from us? Do we not know that they would love to share with us what God is doing in the house churches (and in many cases in the TSPM churches)? Can we not see that this is the way the system works, and that to accept the only voice you are allowed to hear — the voice of that narrow band of TSPM leaders at the top of the pyramid — automatically harms the house churches right across China, with their millions of believers? No wonder the TSPM official magazine claims that "they have lit a fire in the backyard" of evangelicals in the West. I rather think that the authorities must be surprised and amused at our gullibility!

I know that it can well be truthfully argued that there is no one unified voice of the house churches in China. I fully accept that, for they are a disparate and sometimes divided group. But a careful approach will persuade us that this is evidence for the genuineness of their voice, rather than against it. That is because their voices generally agree in what they share with us, constituting a chorus in harmony out of diversity!

3. A stark challenge to the reader.

Do you know that it was easier for Billy Graham to witness about Jesus to the Marxist Premier of China that it was for him to hear the real truth about the house churches from a Christian leader in China?

In April 1988, when Billy Graham visited China, he was allowed to visit Li Peng — even to share the Gospel with him. That is good, and we may see it as God's mercy, seeking to divert that man from the atrocity that he was to commit a year later.

But Billy Graham was not allowed to visit with Xu Yongze. Xu is a house church leader from central China, with a large number of churches in the movement that he leads. He came to Beijing specifically to meet with Billy Graham, to try to help the American evangelist to hear clearly that other voice — the voice of the house churches in China. Xu wanted to be sure that this godly leader from the West really understood the situation in China from the point of view of the house churches. He was not sure that Graham would hear it from those he was going to see in China.

But Xu Yongze never got to see Billy Graham. He was plucked off the streets by the security police and has not been seen since — in spite of questions from Billy Graham himself and from the US Embassy. Under normal circumstances, a man cannot legally be held for longer than two, or at most three, months in China. But Xu has not been tried yet, at least so far as we know. A fellow worker who visited him was also arrested for trying to carry out a message from him.

What a challenge that presents to evangelical leaders outside China. Do you realise that it could be easier for you to see the Premier of all China, Li Peng, and to share the Gospel with him, than it is for you to hear from a major spiritual leader in China about the house church situation in that country? Surely we must see what is going on, and be wiser than we have been. There are days coming when the continued revival in the house churches in China may in part depend on that.

There is little doubt in my mind that it is the house churches which are the mainstream of Christianity in China. It is they who are genuinely seeking to follow the 'Three Self' principles set out by John Nevius so many years ago. As such they are more than deserving of our attention, our prayer and our assistance.

We then have to go back to old brother Wang Mingdao in Shanghai, radiant in his love of the Lord, though old and infirm in body. I asked him what he would like to share with his brothers and sisters in the West. It was simply that "Jesus said to His disciples that they should not fear. Many stumble, but the commonest cause of stumbling is the fear of man. Jesus told us to believe, to trust in Him, not to fear . . . In the 1960's I was told that I was near to death, but here I am today. God has provided all that I have needed to serve Him". Such a testimony to the faithfulness of God moves our hearts — especially when we know that it cost him 23 years in prison to see it so deeply forged into his life and experience. The most fruitful years of his ministry were lost, because of TSPM betrayal. Dare we really not make every effort to hear what men like that are saying?

There is more than polemic to be heard there. The essence of the house church movement in China is there — a story of deep spiritual well springs. On one trip to

China God spoke to me from Psalm 27:13-14, as a summary of brother Wang and of many, many leaders and Christians in the house church movement in China: "I am still confident of this: I will see the goodness of the Lord in the land of the living. Wait for the Lord; be strong and take heart and wait for the Lord."

They have had so little, these Christians. They have faced so much. And yet, as they walked in faith in the goodness of God, they have proved His love again and again. There is an amazing stream of genuine spiritual life flowing amongst them, an addition to Hebrews 11 written before our eyes by the power of God.

It takes us back to Renguang and Enhui in Shanghai: *"Please be a reporter for us"*, they said, *"We have no means by which our voice can be heard by others, inside or outside of China. Simply say to our brothers and sisters outside of China: 'Some people tell one story, and their voice is heard. But others are telling a different story, and their voice is not being heard'."*

I can share with you what little I know of that other voice in China's church today, the house church voice and testimony. I can try to attune you to the sound of that deep heartcry from those sons and daughters of the living God. I can point you to others who know much more than I do, who can help you better than I to listen and to hear. But I cannot make you. That is up to you — before men and before God.

CHAPTER 6

THE HIDDEN POWER —
PRAYING FOR CHINA

Paul Kauffman of Asian Outreach has observed that we
will never understand why the Chinese church has grown
so much, and still is continuing to see revival in some
parts, until we understand the place of prayer in the
corporate and individual lives of Chinese Christians.
After 1949, leaders were removed, imprisoned or killed.
They also saw the removal and departure of the entire
missionary force. Foreigners with a deep love for China
could do nothing for her as they watched from abroad
— except pray. And pray they did. National leaders,
restricted or imprisoned, could do nothing — except
pray. And pray they did. Many in the churches were left
with little they could or dared do — except pray. And
pray they did. No wonder China is seeing revival today!

But that was not a temporary phenomenon. Prayer
remains a vital key in the life of the Chinese church. A
friend told me how he was driven through the night to
speak at some meetings deep in the countryside in
China. The rather imperfect vehicle in which they were
travelling broke down in the middle of the night, and

they were still some way from their destination. The brethren tried to mend it, but it did not respond. So they laid hands on it and prayed — and off they went. God had done what man could not, and got the vehicle going again. When they arrived at about 5am, he was told that he should rest — he would be speaking through the day — many leaders had come, hungry to hear God's word expounded. But his Chinese brethren did not rest — they went off to attend a 5.30am prayer meeting! The fact that they had just driven through a large part of the night did not seem important. They simply believed at that point that they needed to seek the blessing of God in prayer more than they needed to sleep.

Yonggi Cho, the pastor of a huge church in South Korea, has said that "one of the greatest lies of Satan is that we just don't have enough time to pray . . . As soon as we realise that prayer is as important as sleeping, eating and breathing, we will be amazed at how much more time will be available to us for prayer . . . It will take violent dedication to prayer to bring the power of God into our lives. This violent earnestness will be most evident in discipline. We must set priorities for our time. Satan opposes the prayers of God's people more than anything else. Our problem has been we have thought about prayer, read about prayer and even received teaching about prayer, but we just haven't prayed."

John Wesley put it this way: "God does nothing redemptively in the world — except through prayer". In meditating on that, Selwyn Hughes has observed that whenever God wants to bring His purposes to pass here on the earth, He does not act arbitrarily, but touches the hearts of praying people — and then ushers in His purposes across the bridge of prayer. God may be sovereign, but He is not capricious or dictatorial. That is why prayer and revival are so inseparably linked. Selwyn Hughes observed that he knows of no revival which was not connected in some way with powerful, believing intercessory prayer. Thus when God decides that a spiritual revival is necessary, He seeks to lay a burden of prayer upon the hearts of His children. He then must find those who are willing to receive it. He has found that in China. He is also looking for it outside of China.

We need to face this challenge. It would be easy — and not untypical — for us to slip off into a discussion along the lines of the chicken and egg. Is it God Who has to move first, prompting and anointing us to pray? Or is it we who need to seek Him first? But in China I suspect they would take another approach. They would simply get on their faces and start crying to God, expecting Him to answer prayer with revival power — and also to sort out the theological questions if He considered it was necessary!

Indeed, it has been reported that some Christians in China were asked what their three priorities would be if they could tell Christians outside China how to help them. Their answer was something like: "Number 1: prayer; Number 2: prayer; Number 3: prayer." In fact I believe that they did add a little bit more — that other Christians should be informed of the need to pray for the church in China, as well as being told actually to do so! But for them there was no other priority. In the opinion of the people asked, prayer and the need to challenge Christians about prayer were the only real priorities.

It is a fact that some Chinese Christians do regularly give extended time to praying for other areas of the world. They intercede with passion and commitment for their brethren, including those of us in the so-called 'free' countries. Given their situation and most urgent needs, that does somewhat put pressure on us to respond in kind!

How should we pray for China?

I would like to be practical, and to suggest specific **areas** of prayer for China — the nation and the church.

1. Pray for the Government.

In 1 Timothy 2:1-6, the apostle Paul instructs us to pray for kings and all in authority, for governments and those who rule the nations. That is very applicable to China. Note that he does say "for" them — not "against" them. That is because He has a specific target in mind. Verse 2 tells us that He wants nations and peoples — the Christians included — to live peaceful and quiet lives. That in turn is for a specific reason. Verse 4 says that God wants all men to be saved. Peaceful conditions in a nation enable Christians to get on with the job that the Master gave them — preaching the Gospel all over their nation. Division of any kind in a nation, especially that caused by bad government (and much of it is, in East and West alike), brings tension, civil strife, and other agendas than the Gospel.

May I ask you to pray for China in that way, asking that God in these days would sovereignly restore peace and quiet to the nation, so that Christians might be able to bring in the harvest of needy people following the recent troubles?

2. Pray for the church.

i) Firstly, for freedom from persecution.

The main reason for this, apart from our love of the brethren in China and the desire that they should not suffer, is again that they should be able to win men, women and children to Christ more freely.

Persecution has been a fact of life for Chinese Christians almost since the birth of the church. Today the Religious Affairs Bureau still carries out policies that are basically hostile to Christianity. In some areas their hostility has intensified. Arrests of believers still take place. A 25 year old woman evangelist gave herself up to the authorities after police had arrested members of a church she had started. The church had become known to the TSPM, who passed on the information to the Public Security Bureau (PSB), who then arrested several leaders of the church. They were released when the woman evangelist gave herself up.

A brief survey of some of the incidents that took place in 1987 will serve to show the extent to which persecution of Christians continues:

- In Jiangsu province, 6 house church leaders connected with the former 'Jesus Family' were arrested and beaten up.

- In Shaanxi province a believer was arrested for travelling with Western Christians. In the same area 40 Christians were detained en masse and 12 house church leaders taken into custody.

- In Henan province a young Christian was arrested at the railway station by police for picking up boxes of Bibles.

- In Guangdong 2 people were arrested for obtaining Bibles and books from another house church.

- In Hunan province a house church leader was arrested and Christians were told by the police not to share their faith, attend meetings, listen to gospel radio, or receive Bibles from overseas.

- In Hebei province 72 house church Christians were arrested while holding a meeting — for refusing to join the TSPM. Two of them were later sentenced to 3 years 're-education through labour'.

These are but a few examples of persecution that continues today. The reasons for arrest are usually as follows: leadership in the house church movement, which is perceived as opposition to the TSPM; contact with Christian organisations or individuals outside of China; distribution of Bibles and books from overseas; mimeographing Christian literature.

The whole issue of persecution, which takes many forms, some more severe than others, is deserving of our thoughts and prayers. Chinese Christians are being denied the basic human right of religious freedom. They are being harassed, detained, arrested, imprisoned, physically abused and restricted and opposed in all their efforts to carry out the Great Commission.

Even those believers who attend TSPM churches are increasingly being brought under pressure. A document recently issued by the United Front Work Department states: "We must draw a clear distinction between the Bible and Party policy. Where the Bible and Party policy conflict, we must unwaveringly implement matters according to Party policy."

It is true that many Christians in China see the positive side of persecution, and regard it as having a purifying effect on the life of the church. As one woman who had experienced considerable difficulty because of her faith said: "If a person joins us, we have a real Christian." This does not mean, however, that we should just sit back and applaud what the authorities are doing. The suffering is real; the heartache of separation from family, friends and loved ones is no easier to bear, even when seen in a positive light.

We need to pray for God's mercy, strength and grace upon the Christians who even now are suffering for Christ's sake.

ii) For those in prison. Hebrews 13:3.
We need to pray for those in detention, and for their families who remain at home suffering, having to make ends meet under very difficult situations. It is sometimes hard to know who suffers most in this type of situation — the prisoner or his family — even though the families of imprisoned believers do often receive a great deal of support from their fellow Christians.

iii) For Christian workers.
Pray for the itinerant evangelists, men and women who are branded as 'illegal' by the authorities, and who often risk their very lives for the sake of being able to spread the gospel and see churches planted in areas that have never heard of Jesus.

Pray for house church and TSPM pastors alike. Some

94

are very ill-trained, some do not even have any materials with which to do their work. Others work under very difficult situations.

iv) For the needs of the church.
Pray for resources to be released from the churches in the outside world that will enable the Chinese church to receive materials for the building up of believers, the training of leaders and the propagating of the truth. More will be said in the following chapters about the ministries of Christian radio broadcasts, and the provision of tapes and literature. Pray that heresy and false teaching will be opposed and defeated, and that the body of Christ might know continued boldness, grace, courage, power and perseverance. Pray for the ministries outside of China, like CCSM, that are committed to providing radio programmes, tapes, Bibles and literature for China.

v) Pray for the relationship between the TSPM and the house churches.
Much has been said already in chapters 4 and 5 on this subject.

vi) Pray for the Catholic church in China.
The Vatican has historically maintained relationships with Taiwan, so that the official Catholic Patriotic Church in China pays no attention to the Vatican or the Pope, appointing its own bishops and running its own churches. Some assess that many Catholics are still loyal to the Vatican, and that there is a Catholic equivalent to the Protestant house church movement in China. Leaders in this section of the church, regarded as unpatriotic, have suffered much. Pray for God's blessing and reviving power on that church.

3. Pray for children and young people in China.
We need not think that it is only the adults who suffer

persecution. A pupil in a primary school wrote on July 29th, 1988: "We are being persecuted. There are five believers in my class. We got permission from my teacher to take time off from school so we could be baptised with 300 other people. When we returned the headmaster was very angry. He asked all the believers to stand up and asked us why we believed in this superstition. After arguing a while he expelled us from the school. Please pray for him."

Pray for the children of believers, who often display amazing boldness, courage, discernment, wisdom and understanding at a very tender age. They are quite willing to suffer for the name of Jesus, but let us pray for God's hand of protection upon them. Pray also for the massive percentage of the population in China who are under 20 years of age. Most do not yet know Christ. Many are disillusioned by recent events — a generation that will seek to make materialism their god unless they first come to faith in Christ.

Pray particularly for the over one million university students in this category, many of whom are deeply wounded and disillusioned by the events in and around Tiananmen Square, and their consequences across the whole country.

4. Pray for the evangelisation of China.

China has a population of over one billion people. Even if there are 50 million believers in China today, that still means there are the better part of that one billion people who are heading for an eternity without the Lord Jesus Christ. 95 percent of the Chinese population is still without Christ and therefore without hope.

There are different sectors of Chinese society that need the Gospel:

i) **The intellectuals** — teachers and students. As so often in the past, they are suffering again. Even before that, many were dissatisfied and unhappy with poor wages and housing — sometimes peasants on the farms earn more than highly qualified university lecturers. Pray that many might turn to Christ — either in China or while studying abroad.

ii) The vast mass of **China's workers** in the cities and "peasants" in the countryside. They need Christ.

iii) The 40-50 million **communist party member**s. These are the elite and the privileged — only a small percentage of the people can be party members. By definition of membership they should not believe in Christ. Pray that many would be saved and serve the Lord Jesus openly, though that is often at great personal cost.

iv) The **military** men and women in China. There are more than three million in China today.

v) The **other religions** — Buddhists, Daoist, Confucianists etc. They run deep in China's culture, and some forms of them have powerful occult roots.

vi) The **unevangelised areas of China.** There are whole peoples who have never been touched with the good news of new life in Christ. Some provinces are remote and unreached largely by the Gospel. Some of the autonomous regions are in deep need — Tibet, Xinjiang (mostly Islamic), Inner Mongolia.

vii) The other **ethnic minorities.**
There are about 50 different tribes (non Han Chinese) in China, actually living in almost 50 percent of the land space — with 50 different languages! Yunnan is said to have 28 ethnic minorities. There are even nearly two million Koreans in China.

viii) The **Han Chinese,** the largest people group in China and therefore where the majority of Christians are to be found. Pray also that they will catch the vision to reach out to the minority groups of their country with the message of God's love and reconciliation.

ix) **Christians** from Hong Kong, other Asian countries, Africa and from many other nations of the world **who work and study in China.** Also for those who go in as businessmen or tourists. Pray for God's

Hand upon them in pastoral help and especially in evangelism.

5. Pray for Hong Kong and Taiwan.

Pray especially that God will grant His help and wisdom in the run up to the Communist takeover of Hong Kong in 1997, when their very existence will be called into question. The Tiananmen massacre has created a very volatile situation in Hong Kong.

★★★★★★★★★★★★★★★★★★★★★★★★

The comments in this chapter are intended to be no more than an introduction to a high calling — praying for China. Here, finally, are a few practical suggestions that will help you to take more steps along the road:

1. Set aside a regular part of your prayer time to pray for China. Be disciplined so that you do not only pray for personal needs or for your own locality or country.

2. Find others who will join together on a regular basis with you to pray for China. Once a week would be a good target to aim for.

3. Get materials to inform and help you to pray. Some suggestions:

i) Buy "Operation World". Patrick Johnstone STL\WEC. (4th Edition). Refer in it to the section on China.

ii) Obtain regular prayer information. The following groups will be helpful, though the list is not exclusive.

1. ASIAN OUTREACH INTERNATIONAL,
    P O Box 3448, HONG KONG.
    "Asian Report."

2. CCCOWE
    19 Mongkok Road, 3rd Fl., Kowloon,
    HONG KONG.
    "Chinese around the World."

3. **CHINESE CHURCH RESEARCH CENTRE,**
   P O Box 312, Shatin Central Post Office,
   Shatin, New Territories, HONG KONG.
   "China and the Church Today".
   Weekly "China News and Church Report".

4. **CHINESE CHURCH SUPPORT MINISTRIES**
   2[b] Carr Lane, Acomb, YORK. YO2 5HU.
   Regular prayer and tape material.

5. **CHRISTIAN COMMUNICATIONS LTD.,**
   P O Box 95364, Tsimshatsui, HONG KONG.
   "Pray for China."

6. **FAR EAST BROADCASTING COMPANY,**
   P O Box 96789, Tsimshatsui, Kowloon,
   HONG KONG
   Monthly prayer group material for China radio.

7. **INSTITUTE OF CHINESE STUDIES:**
   U.S. CENTRE FOR WORLD MISSIONS
   P O Box 1170, Monterey Park, CA. 91754, USA.
   "Watchmen on the Great Wall."

8. **OVERSEAS MISSIONARY FELLOWSHIP,**
   P O Box 70505, Kowloon Central Post Office,
   Kowloon, HONG KONG.
   (Also with branches in many countries.)
   "Pray for China Fellowship" monthly prayer
   material (Highly recommended).

Chinese Church Support Ministries can help if you
require further advice. Please write to the address above.

CHAPTER 7

MIGHTIER THAN THE SWORD

A Christian organisation was celebrating inside China a special event a few years ago — the millionth piece of Christian literature that they had given to their beloved brethren in China. A godly old pastor took a tea cup and spilt some tea on the dry earth on which he stood. He thanked them for all that they had done — but he asked them to remember that all they had given in the way of Bibles and Christian books was as a drop of water on a dry and thirsty land.

There is a desperate shortage of Bibles and Christian literature in China. The TSPM have given the impression in the West that Bibles and other Christian literature materials are no longer needed. One of the reasons suggested is that sufficient Bibles are being printed on the Amity printing press to meet the needs of Chinese Christians. That is not accurate. Story after story from the house churches speaks of the urgent need for materials of every kind.

Letters received from China give some indication of the tremendous need — a rather different picture than the one which the TSPM has sometimes given. It brings us back to the question of which voice we are hearing, of whose is the real heartcry of China's church.

"It is God who gives strength. We lack preachers. The Christians are new babes in Christ. Bibles are insufficient. Many are copied by hand. Without spiritual materials the ministry is very difficult. Many scripture passages need to be understood. I pray that you would increase our spiritual materials to help us in our study of the Bible."

"Our spiritual lives are still childish and dry, urgently needing a lot of spiritual food and nourishment. We request that you send us books and teaching materials."

"We are still very far from being close to our Lord, and are very unclear about the mysteries of the Bible. We still don't have anyone who truly understands these mysteries. We are really lacking! You see how pained we are in our heart, always longing for the Lord to send spiritual spring and autumn rains, to irrigate my thirsty heart...please satisfy my spiritual longing, please! I ask you to send me several spiritual books . . ."

This is but a small sample of the type of letters that are constantly received by China ministries. There is such a huge dearth of good Christian literature in China, and the believers are almost at the point of begging for help from their fellow believers outside of China.

In this chapter, I want briefly to tackle the question of the real situation about Christian literature in China by asking three questions.

1. What is the real situation concerning Christian literature in China today?

I think that it is best to divide the answer to that into two separate categories — firstly, Bibles and then other Biblical teaching materials.

(i) What really is the position concerning Bibles in China today?

I have spoken elsewhere about the good work being done by the Amity Press in Nanjing on behalf of the TSPM, producing Bibles in increasing numbers. But we need to see it as only a part of the answer. Simple mathematics should tell us why that is so. Please consider carefully with me the following line of reasoning:

. . . Suppose there are 50 million believers in China today.

. . . Suppose also that one million Bibles are provided for China by any and all sources each year — either printed by Amity or carried in from Hong Kong and elsewhere. (That number of one million would be, at the time of writing, twice as many as Amity have produced in total from the time that they went into production until now).

. . . How long then would it take, at that rate, to give every believer now alive in China a Bible. The answer is simple — 50 years.

But there are three problems there.

. . . Firstly, how would all the new Christians who need Bibles get one each — those Christians who will come to Christ in the 50 years that it takes to get today's Christians one Bible each. As soon as we have finished getting Bibles to today's Christians, we will have to start all over again for the new ones! There were only about one million Protestant believers in 1949 when the Communists came to power, and now there are 50 million. If the Lord tarries, we may assume that the numbers will grow by more than that in the next fifty years. After fifty years of taking one million Bibles a year into China we will be further behind than we are now!

. . . Secondly, do not unbelieving Chinese have the right to read the word of God if they wish to? What about the other 950,000,000 or more people who might want to read the Bible? That means more Bibles are needed than ever.

. . . Thirdly, what about the minority groups that we have mentioned in the chapter on prayer above. Over fifty different groupings, many of which need the Scriptures in their own ethnic languages. Millions upon millions of Muslims, in different dialects and languages, as well as Koreans, Yi, Li, Yao and Lisu and many more.

Enough. The point should be clear by now. China needs Bibles.

On top of that, many Bibles never actually reach the hands of those who are most desperate for them. In some rural areas, where Christianity is growing at the fastest rate, several hundred believers can share one Bible. At the same time the Public Security Police generally try to prevent the provision of Bibles and other materials from abroad, even entering people's homes in an attempt to discover and confiscate such materials. On occasions, TSPM pastors have been involved in such raids.

Recent evidence points to the random searching of trains inside China, and the detention of those found carrying Bibles. It is clear that those who most need the Bibles find them hardest to obtain.

It is very hard to imagine just how difficult it is for many Chinese Christians to obtain a Bible. Just think what a relatively simple task it is for anyone in the West to buy a copy. Perhaps the inconvenience of a car ride to the centre of town, to the nearest bookshop, is the greatest obstacle we have to overcome. It is doubtful if the cost is a great problem, as there are so many versions available at reasonable prices. There is certainly no risk involved. At the very most, it will entail crossing the road in busy traffic! Altogether it is a minor task for most of us, involving very little effort, time or money.

For a Chinese believer, the story is completely different. Obtaining a Bible could mean travelling for several days and putting oneself at risk simply for trying to get hold of a copy of God's word.

In many churches there are simply not enough Bibles to go around. It is normal to share the Scriptures, but this does hinder people's spiritual growth, as they are not able to study as regularly as they would like. Imagine how often you would see a Bible if you were sharing it with one hundred other people.

Because many of the house churches do not wish to obtain any copies of the Bible from TSPM sources, they will often decide to send a member of their congregation to one of the larger cities. This will usually be as the result of someone having a contact there who can supply Bibles from abroad. A collection will be taken up from all of the believers to pay for travel and other expenses. There will be sacrificial giving on the part of all concerned. The member chosen to go and obtain the Bibles will set out for the city, which could be two days' train journey away. Two days on a hard wooden seat, with nowhere to sleep.

For the particular member it may be the first time out of his home village, and once in the city, he will doubtless feel intimidated by the hustle and bustle of city life. As a complete stranger he also has to find the contact whom he hopes will give him the Bibles for which he has come so far. There is certainly no guarantee that he will receive the quantity of Bibles he wishes to purchase, or even that there will be any available.

If he receives the Bibles, he will immediately return to his village two days journey away, praying both for protection on the way and that his mission will not be discovered by the authorities. But the risks will have been worthwhile when he can present the newly obtained copies of God's word to the pastors and members of his church. There will be great rejoicing, and sometimes tears shed for the joy of being able to let more members have a Bible.

Even when the mission is successfully accomplished, the joy might be short lived, for such is the rate of growth in many of the churches that they will soon be back to sharing the Bible between many once again. The answer? To make another long, risky, expensive journey to obtain more Bibles from the contact whom he hopes has received sufficient quantities from abroad to be able to meet their need.

Such a situation is very common among the house churches today. In a certain village, about 80 people came to know the Lord, but only had 3 Bibles between them. They took it in turns to read a copy, but between these rare moments they would write down everything that the preacher said, in order to try and assimilate God's word more quickly.

In another area, believers had to resort to hand copying the Bible. There were 60,000 believers in the district, with only six reference Bibles between them. These Bibles were thirty years old and written in the old script, which many found very difficult to understand. People took it in turns to borrow a Bible and copy the scriptures by hand every day, often working so long that their fingers were swollen.

It is true that in the larger cities, where one or more of the 5,000 or more open TSPM churches exist, Christians can buy Bibles from the TSPM. But some house churches hold back from that for various reasons — for example, there is a fear of a detailed registration form having to be completed if a Bible is wanted.

One incident that sticks in my mind occurred in a major city of China last year. We were sharing with a godly old house church pastor. He told us, in the course of our talking, that he had lost his cross-reference Bible. Cross-reference Bibles are very valuable preaching tools, and this would represent a major loss to this dear and proven servant of God. The Chinese expression for a cross reference Bible is a "string of pearls Bible". Evidently this brother, like many others, saw it as having the same value as a real string of pearls! The means of his losing it was fascinating. He had put in down on a table in the church after preaching, and it had been stolen — with the thief leaving behind his scruffy old ordinary Bible. We may not agree with the ethics, but at least it shows a hunger! Imagine our joy to be able to come the next day with several new cross-reference Bibles that we had just brought in from Hong Kong! What a privilege it was to serve this old man of God in such a special way.

(ii) What about other forms of Christian literature — foundational teaching materials, concordances, apologetic and teaching materials etc?

Over the last few years, the requests from various house church groups have focussed as much on the need for teaching materials about the Bible as they have on the Bibles themselves. That is not because the Chinese believers in any way feel the Bible is not sufficient, or that it is not the word of God. It is simply that they are experiencing great pressures from a lack of training, and also from heresy.

Dennis Balcombe, a highly respected colleague with an unparalleled love for the Chinese churches and people, showed me some materials that had come from central China. One letter was describing the danger of heresy from within the church in the writer's area. Of such people, the writer wrote as follows: *"I must say they are doing much harm to the evangelistic work of X district. They publicly deny the Old Testament, and fallaciously interpret and revise the New Testament"*. The rest of the letter reveals the deep needs of the believers in the area, and the ways in which the false teachers were *"through all these proclamations, injecting anaesthetics into the believers' hearts"*. Dennis told me that the confusion had led the people in that area, even though they were in the midst of revival, to stop winning souls to Christ. But when good strong Biblical teaching was brought to them, they responded warmly and quickly.

Chinese Church Support Ministries is much involved in this kind of work. We are actively involved in translating key Christian books and publishing them for China in special compact editions. We have worked with

Derek Prince Ministries to produce vital books from Derek's anointed teaching — the first 10,000 copies of his special China version "Self Study Bible Course" disappeared into China in a few months. We are involved in that because God spoke to me several years ago of the need to take such foundational materials into China. Revival, if it is to continue to grow and to spread, must see the work of the Spirit of God rooted into the Bible — the word of God. What an investment we can make in China today, where the Spirit of God is working so powerfully.

2. Do the materials do any good once they are taken into China?

Bibles and reference materials taken into China by couriers have been one of the key aspects in the spread of the revival, particularly in rural areas. The Bibles are often distributed over a very wide area within days of being taken over the border. One elderly house church evangelist in Yunnan province travels hundreds of miles to take scriptures and books to remote, but often very large, groups of Christians in the mountainous areas.

The Bibles themselves act as missionaries, and cause the revival to spread, thus creating an even greater need for more Bibles. In one district, itinerant evangelists visited a village that had 300 believers. They had little literature with them, but gave them what they had — a few Bibles. They returned less than a year later to find that the number of believers had grown to 800.

In Southern China I heard a most encouraging story from a house church pastor, showing how God can bless and use even the most unlikely plans. Farmers with paddy fields near the sea one day found that bags of books had been washed up on to the shore. They were not especially interested in the contents, and possibly assumed that they might be political propaganda. In any case they thought of a good use for the books, which were sealed tightly in plastic bags and had obviously been floated in on the tide. The farmers used them as building blocks to build up the banks of their paddy fields!

So it might have remained, except that a Christian happened to be visiting a friend in the fields one day. He apparently trod on one of the bags by accident, and being of a curious nature, opened it. Imagine his amazement to find these piles of Bibles, mostly still in good condition, wrapped as they were in the water tight bags in which they had floated on to the beach. A small commercial deal was quickly arranged — the farmers wanted some recompense for the damage to their paddy field walls caused by the removal of the Bible "blocks"!

But there was a sting in the tail. The house church pastor informed me, with joy in his heart, that the Bibles were no longer in the area — they had been distributed to needier areas in different parts of China!

Such is the power of God's word. Such is the need. Such is the opportunity for Christians outside of China to help their brethren inside.

This is China today. So many of our efforts are but sprinkles of water on a dry, weary and thirsty land. But we are at least trying to do something.

3. What can be done and who is doing it?

Various China ministries are doing all they can, with the limited resources that they have, to meet the needs. Thousands of foreigners and Hong Kong Chinese cross the border into China regularly, and through one agency alone, over 3 million Bibles, New Testaments and other books have been passed to Chinese Christians. A few of these couriers have been arrested, but most are released after a few hours questioning, and the longest detention to date has been five days. But they have the joy and thrill of knowing that they have placed something of inestimable value into the hands of those who are crying out for it.

But the need is so great that, even with the volume of traffic there is at present, the task is too big for any one organisation. There can never be enough material taken over to feed the spiritual hunger of China's believers. In 1987, 57 percent of all letters written to the Far Eastern Broadcasting Company asked for Bibles, and 35 percent asked for other spiritual books.

It is heartbreaking to know that so many who are hoping and relying on Christians outside of China will be disappointed because there simply is not enough material available at present. There are believers in China today who want to preach the gospel, start churches and distribute Bibles, but they do not have the necessary materials.

After a meeting in Henan province, a worker from one of the China ministries based in Hong Kong saw leaders of house churches come asking for Bibles. Some of them represented groups of a thousand or more believers, but all they could be given was two or three books each. Some wept at that disappointment. How could they pastor their large flocks with so little spiritual nourishment?

A group of pastors from the north of China came looking for Bibles, stating that they needed three or four thousand copies for their workers. When told that they could only have 3 or 4 copies each, they wept. They had come with many bags and suitcases in which to take the books back, but returned with these empty. After being given the news of the scarcity of Bibles, they wept through the night. They had been sent on a mission by their churches, and would have to go back and report that they were unable to obtain the Bibles they so urgently needed.

Another sister came with the news that there was only one Bible between 120 believers in her area, and only one reference Bible for 20 pastors. On being told that there were none available to her, she refused to return home, but stayed, fasted and prayed that God would intervene. Four days later sufficient quantities arrived for her needs.

There is a relatively open door to supply literature at this time. The present policies of the Chinese Government make this possible. The problem is that interest in China often falls short of positive action. There is a much wider need for many kinds of Christian literature: teaching materials for leaders; nurture materials for young Christians; evangelistic and apologetic books for a generation that has been taught that science is god and religion is empty, yet who know deep within themselves that it is their own hearts and lives that are empty; childrens' materials and much more.

I need to bring it nearer home by asking a further question: what can British, American, Australasian and other Christians do? Let me suggest three practical steps:

1. Intercede for those involved in carrying literature over the border and for the couriers from house churches inside China.

2. Personally help to carry Bibles and other literature over, perhaps as a vacation experience.

3. Help by financial support to this vital ministry.

CCSM can advise and help by recommending specific organisations who are engaged in these ministries, and who fall into the three categories mentioned above. We are working in close association with a number of other ministries who have a particular burden for China. Please write to us if you desire help to do something practical in these areas.

The opportunity is there to do something of eternal value for China. The situation will never arise where there are too many couriers wanting to go across the border. There will never be more than enough finance to produce all the material that is required, nor enough prayer offered up to the throne of God on behalf of those involved in this ministry.

Isaiah 58:7 tells us of one aspect of the fast that is pleasing to God:

"Is it (the kind of fast that God Himself has chosen) not to share your food with the hungry?"

Who is prepared to share their food with the hungry?

CHAPTER 8

VOICES OF LOVE
FROM OVER THE WALL

In a district of China called Ping Yu Xian there were thought to be no Christians at all. An itinerant evangelist visited there. Much to his surprise and delight, he found there were 1,000 believers. Although overjoyed at what he found, he was somewhat perplexed because, as far as he knew, no-one had been in the district to evangelise. When he started to ask questions, he found that all of the believers had been converted as a result of listening to gospel broadcasts on the radio.

The Far Eastern Broadcasting Company (FEBC) reported that in the last four months of 1987 they received over 7,000 responses from within China to their programmes, as many as for the whole of the previous year. The last 5 months of 1988 saw an aggregate number of response letters from China that was the second highest number in the history of FEBC's work for the equivalent period. Letters repeatedly tell of the value of Christian radio ministry, as Christians are fed and encouraged and strengthened in the Lord.

Yet it was not always so. For many years, ministries

113

such as FEBC and TWR (Trans World Radio) broadcast into China not knowing what effect their programmes were having. It was too difficult and dangerous for the Chinese listeners to respond. What a venture of faith those early years were for the Christian radio pioneers. Was anyone listening; did anybody care?

In 1945, a Chinese Christian was captivated by the vision of gospel radio reaching his fellow Chinese. He approached the government of the time, and was given permission to use a small 500 watt station in Shanghai. When the Communists came to power, however, he was labelled an enemy of the people, and his Christian radio station confiscated.

Little did he realise that his vision was being fulfilled from outside of China. FEBC, which had been founded in 1945, had built stations in the Philippines, a few hundred miles from the shores of China. In 1946, they had sent their first representative to Shanghai to try and obtain franchises for such an undertaking within China from the Nationalist Government of the time.

The grandson of Hudson Taylor spent many weeks accompanying the representative to a number of government offices, with no success. The Communist armies were already gaining more and more power, and the authorities understood both the value and the dangers of radio, and were reluctant to permit radio stations to be run by private organisations.

With the Communist takeover in 1949, and the retreat of the Nationalist Government to Taiwan, the entire nation of China was cut off from the outside world — except for the voice of radio. No more missionaries were allowed into the country. The church faced almost unprecedented persecution. Almost every means of bringing the gospel to the Chinese people was blocked. But in God's providence, the age of radio had come. The technology was there. The need was there. The first overseas Chinese Christian transmission had been broadcast on July 29th, 1949, just two months before the Communists seized power. Radio now remained virtually the only vehicle by which the gospel could be brought from outside the nation to the unsaved millions and to the needy Christians.

For ten years there was very little response to the programmes, as Communist censorship became more and more effective. Very few listeners dared to write to the radio station, because of the danger of being found out.

As the years went by, FEBC took a further step of faith. They established a studio and research centre in Hong Kong in order to gather as much information as possible about the situation in China. In this way they were better able to prepare programmes that were tailored to meet the needs of their Chinese listeners.

During the chaotic years of the Cultural Revolution, censorship of the post became even tighter, and the few letters that did get through described the tragic conditions prevailing at the time. During the period 1969-1978, FEBC received only 177 responses from its listeners in China, an average of 18 per year. In 1979, after China and the USA had resumed diplomatic relations and the door of China had swung slightly wider, 3,071 letters were received, with a yearly total thereafter of around 10,000.

In the recent years of 1987 and 1988, the total number of letters has been around 16,000 a year, proving just how much impact gospel radio continues to have on China. Bear in mind that many listeners never write. FEBC noticed an almost total absence of responses from one area. But they later discovered that the reason was not that folk did not listen — many in fact did. It was because the church leaders advised the believers not to write — it was too dangerous. Others do write, but their letters are intercepted and never get through. There have been some who have written many times before the letters have reached Hong Kong. The responses received in Hong Kong, though encouraging enough, cannot fully represent the enormous value of the Christian radio ministries into China.

It is a vital way of reaching China's vast population with the gospel. Over the last few years, with the increasing freedoms, more and more individuals own radios, and there is evidence of a real spiritual hunger. It is estimated that 95 percent of Chinese people actually listen to the radio and, in the climate of recent years, believers have had more courage to write to the radio stations and express their opinions, thus helping to improve the quality of the programmes that are broadcast. This means that they are able to listen to programmes that are more suited to their needs and which help them to grow spiritually.

Letters express thanks, and also indicate the deep hunger there is in many areas for the word of God:

"I listen to your gospel broadcast every afternoon and night. Sometimes I have to bring my radio to the field. I rely on your broadcast to shepherd the church. This is because we do not have any spiritual books. All our brothers and sisters are grateful to the Lord for your broadcast. They all agree that not a church here can explain the Bible in a way as precise as yours."

"Brothers and sisters in Christ are unable to study in local theological seminaries because their educational level is not up to par. We shepherd the church by listening to gospel broadcasts. There are still many who have never heard about the gospel."

"My father and mother are blind. They accepted Jesus during the Cultural Revolution. At that time, everywhere in the country was in chaos and people were living in fear. Even the blind could not escape criticism. Although Pa and Ma were criticised all the day, they did not give up listening to your programmes at night. Thank God for the gospel broadcast — a means to spread the gospel which no-one can obstruct."

"Several months ago I saved some money to buy a portable radio. When I am on my way to work or home, I listen to your radio programme. Even though I am having lunch, I will listen to it for at least half an hour. Surprisingly my earnest attitude has moved some of my colleagues. At lunch time we listen together. When they go back home, they continue to listen."

"In order to listen to your programmes I saved money to buy a radio. I benefited a lot from your programmes. I listened and learnt hard day and night without ceasing. My parents were so worried that they warned me to take rest regularly. However, as I thirst for the word of God, I care not for my health and their advice. Only when I have studied hard spiritual matters can I nurture the believers."

Let me try and answer some of the obvious question about radio work.

Question 1: what are the Christian radio ministries into China trying to achieve?

FEBC have for many years had a vision to reach otherwise unreachable areas by radio. They have three main targets in their strategic radio ministry:

i). Training Christian leaders.
Many of China's Christian leaders have come through the Cultural Revolution and though strong in the faith, are elderly. Other leaders are young and recently converted. They are very zealous for the Lord, but they often lack any kind of formal, consistent, biblical training. Sometimes Christians with only a few months experience are asked to take leadership positions in churches. This is not an ideal situation, as it can so easily lead to heresy and false doctrine.

You will remember my sharing about brother Jang's comment to me earlier in this book: *"I have many young people who long to be able to serve Jesus effectively, but I cannot train them because I do not have the personnel or the materials to do so. I cannot send them to the TSPM theological seminaries, because the content is too political. Nor can I send them abroad, for to do so would mean that their records would be marked".* Radio is one of the ways in which we can help in such situations. Certain radio programmes, even blocks of time at certain stages of the day, are set aside for this specific purpose of training present and future leaders.

ii) Nurturing new Christians. This is extremely important because of the lack of Bibles and suitable Christian literature. Groups that have got into false teaching can so easily lead new converts astray. For some believers the radio broadcasts are the only source of help and spiritual nourishment they receive. For geographical and other reasons they have no church or pastor, so the broadcasts have to become both to them.

iii) Evangelising the lost — reaching out over the airwaves to those who do not yet know Jesus. There is a discernible spiritual hunger in China today. Marxism has failed to meet the deepest needs of the people, and they are looking for an ideology that will satisfy. As 80% of the population lives in rural areas, away from the cities and formal churches, radio is often the only means of reaching them.

Among the responses that FEBC receives, about 50% come from unbelievers wanting to know more about Jesus. Each person who writes risks persecution by the authorities for writing. But letters such as those quoted below continue to come in:

"I must thank God for giving me the opportunity to know Him and accept Him as my Saviour through your broadcasts. My attitude towards life has changed and life becomes meaningful and valuable to me."

"Having listened to your programmes since last year, my

118

spiritual life has grown.....my heart is full of joy now because I have found the greatest hope of life through accepting Christ."

A good proportion of responses from listeners in China mention that they became interested in Christianity after listening to gospel broadcasts. These require a great deal of follow up work, and the workers in Hong Kong who undertake this task require much wisdom and strength to get through the heavy workload.

Question 2: are there difficulties in the China radio ministries?

Like any ministry that God is blessing, we would expect opposition from the enemy of the souls of men. The main weapon used by the devil is opposition to listening to the programmes. Some listeners are persecuted by the authorities for listening to radio broadcasts from Hong Kong. This especially has been so in the revival areas like Henan — probably because the authorities are only too aware of the powerful effect that Christian radio broadcasts are having upon the communities. Recently in one area a vehicle drove around issuing public warnings against listening to the broadcasts! Radios have been confiscated in some cases. One young man wrote:

"I have accepted Jesus for about one year. Formerly I did not have a right concept of God. However, I was drawn gradually to God after listening to your programmes. Several days ago I was summoned to the police station to write down how I had got to listen to your broadcasts. The policemen re-emphasised that I had to understand the seriousness of the problem. Then I was asked to swear not to listen to your programmes and write to you any more. The Bibles you gave me were confiscated and have not been returned."

Another area of difficulty that the Christian broadcasting stations face is that of problems in broadcast reception. This can be because of atmospheric conditions (the summer is usually worse for radio waves) or because of the general eleven year cycle of quality of some radio frequencies. There is a human side to that too — the summer months, particularly the harvest months, see the Christians having to work longer hours in the fields, and therefore being at home less to hear the broadcasts.

Again, FEBC, TWR and the other groups face problems in the areas of staff and finance. Skilled workers are needed in various fields — technical and language skills, letter responses, programme preparation and so on. The programmes are expensive too, involving costly equipment in terms of broadcasting facilities.

Finally, there is the problem of the future of Hong Kong. I will deal with this later in the book. Suffice it to say that FEBC and TWR have vital bases in Hong Kong. They also have a good deal of convenient postal and personal interchange through the territory. It is most unlikely that post-1997 Hong Kong, in the hands of the Mainland Chinese, will see a climate that welcomes or allows them to continue.

Question 3: do I personally feel that radio is a strategic ministry for China?

One day in 1984, as I often did at that time, I was walking along York Racecourse meditating and praying. I hasten to say that it was on the days when there were no races! As I listened to the Lord, I heard him speak quite distinctly. "Take Derek Prince into China" were the instructions I received.

At that time I did not know Derek Prince personally, but was aware and appreciative of his ministry and teaching gift. In obedience I approached him, and told him what I felt God was asking me to do. Together we agreed that some of his teaching material should be broadcast into China. I then approached the Far Eastern Broadcasting Company about the possibility of taking in Derek's material. I was in Hong Kong at the time, and left some English sample tapes with the Reverend Ken Lo, the director and vital man on the China side of

FEBC's work. I then travelled into China on one of my visits, giving me the exact environment to pray that Ken would be clear in what God was saying. On my return to Hong Kong I discovered that Ken felt that it was right to proceed. In that way I became personally responsible for regular programmes into China.

Derek Prince has a unique teaching gift. When Derek explains the word of God on a particular subject, the listener may feel that what Derek has said is obvious — until he realises that he did not understand it until Derek opened God's word to him with such clarity. He was a faculty member at King's college Cambridge (where he had been a scholar himself) at the outbreak of the Second World War. He was far from God. But God met him, saved him and turned his life around. He never returned to teach at Cambridge after the war, though he was pressed by his college to do so. Since that time he has travelled the world teaching the word of God. It has indeed been a privilege to work together for the kingdom with Derek and his wife, Ruth.

The system I worked out with FEBC for the Derek Prince materials was simple. Derek's office in the States would send me his "Today with Derek Prince" materials in printed form. David Selby, the International Director of the ministry and husband of Anna, one of Derek's daughters, took responsibility to provide that. One of the joys of serving God is that there are side benefits — friendships with people of quality like David and Anna! The transcripts they sent us are the English radio broadcasts by Derek that have been much used of God in the States, New Zealand and other countries. My job in the UK was to prepare them for the FEBC office in Hong Kong. That meant checking for suitability of material, breaking each one down in outline form and removing all Western references.

The success of that work can be seen in two ways. Firstly, a knowledgeable and very well connected China ministry colleague told me once that the brethren in

China thought that Ye Guangming (Derek's Chinese name in the broadcasts meaning "Clear Light") was Chinese — so totally had I, with FEBC's help, removed all references to the personal background of this man who attended Eton and Cambridge, served in the British army, and now has a worldwide ministry based in Jerusalem and the USA!

Secondly, FEBC were so appreciative of the material in this first broadcast (under the title of *"Living Sacrifice"* from Rom 12:1-2) that Ken Lo approached me to produce a second programme of Derek's material. This second one was to be specifically designed and prepared for training house church leaders in China. The material was once again to be prepared by my office in York and then translated and broadcast by FEBC into China as *"The Workman God Approves"* — from Paul's instructions to Timothy in 2 Timothy 2:15.

While I was thrilled at the thought of being involved in that kind of vital ministry into China, it did raise a problem for me. My own preparatory responsibilities for *"Living Sacrifice"* had put a strain on my ministry and time. I had to prepare and edit one week of Derek's material for each week of the year. With growing involvement in other aspects of the ministry, I found that really began to weigh heavily.

I can remember taking my girls to ballet, and sitting through the class (hearing the bangings and crashing — or should I say delicate tiptoeing — of the young ladies upstairs) while I sat downstairs and edited scripts for China to meet the deadline, trying to shut out the noise of the other parents chatting. I wonder how many of those parents realised that thousands of people would hear the results of what this busy but silent parent was doing beneath the tap dancing and ballet classes above! Equally, if I went out of town on ministry or holiday for a few days or longer, there was a double load waiting for me when I got back. It was too much.

I felt that my calling was to open up new ground, not

to be tied down under that load. Subsequent events have proved me right, for the whole area of literature for China only opened up after I had laid aside that weekly radio responsibility.

But God had an amazing provision in store. I came to the point, when FEBC asked us to do the second programme *"The Workman God Approves"*, of saying to the Lord that either He provided help or I felt I could not go on. Valerie Dean, working for me in CCSM, suggested that I try contacting a friend of hers, Sue Wooff. Sue is Australian, and brought with her the exact training required. She has received training from both a Bible school and Secretarial College. But Sue is more than that. She also brings personal qualities of great value — a deep love for the Lord and the ability to take responsibility for a job and get it done. Sue is one of that rare breed of people who just gets on with it. If she needs advice or help she comes to me; if she needs to work more, she does it. Lord, give us more Sue Wooffs amongst the labourers in Your kingdom!

The responses from China to both programmes (*"Living Sacrifice"* and *"The Workman God Approves"*) have been extremely encouraging. *"The Workman God Approves"* became the twelfth most popular programme broadcast by FEBC in terms of written responses in 1987 — its first full year of production. *'Living Sacrifice'* has, or is now, being beamed into China in a number of dialects apart from the standard Mandarin Chinese.

The radio ministry has brought great joy to me. The Hand of God has been so clearly in it. It has been a great joy to work with men like Ken Lo and Peter Tong (the programme director) of FEBC. It is a real privilege to count them as co-labourers and personal friends. They are men who have thrown aside other more lucrative opportunities in Hong Kong in order to serve the Lord and the church in China with great skill and dedication. They are worthy of our support and prayer.

The fellowship with Derek Prince ministries has been

123

wonderful, as I have worked within the organisation as the director of the China Outreach side of the programme. Derek himself took responsibility for the heavy financial burden that this work involves — it is a Derek Prince Ministries and not a Chinese Church Support Ministries project. The costs are high for Derek Prince Ministries — many thousands of US dollars a year — for translation, airing and production. Yet Derek and Ruth, with David Selby, have embraced that financial burden gladly to serve God's people in China. Others might have said that the world-wide ministry of DPM had enough responsibilities and burdens to keep them busy. They did not. God had spoken; they needed to respond in faith and obedience; and they did.

Countless millions are passing into a Christless eternity. Working in this team together, we desire to give those millions the opportunity through radio to hear of the love of God; to be built up in that love through His word; and, as God calls, to help them to be teachers of others.

There is always room for people to be involved in this important ministry. Radio stations require scriptwriters who can produce material for China, programme producers, announcers, engineers, administrators and other personnel. And, of course, there is always a need for prayer and finance to support the ongoing work.

Once again, the opportunities are there if people are willing to seek God concerning what He might want them to do with their gifts and abilities.

Christian teaching tapes for China.

In addition to the radio ministry, there is also another related and very effective way of providing teaching material for the church in China. It is by providing teaching and other Christian tapes in Chinese, and taking them in to the believers.

Under the Four Modernisations Programme, modern electronic equipment has become much more readily available, including tape recorders. This has provided an opening for the distribution and use of Christian tape material.

Master tapes of preaching and other Christian material can be taken in to China, placed at strategic locations, and then copied within local Christian networks — for wide distribution among believers.

This method of distributing material has some distinct advantages over even radio programmes. The radio has to be listened to at a particular time and without interruption. The programme cannot be repeated if a part of the message is missed, and the programmes are sometimes affected by poor reception or breakdown of the transmitters.

One tape master can be duplicated many times and widely distributed. The tape can then be listened to whenever and wherever the listener requires, and played over many times to get fuller understanding. In many areas, literacy is a problem, especially among the older members of the population, and tapes overcome the need to read.

There are many valuable projects that need to be undertaken in the tape ministry for China. For example, tapes of hymns, for China's Christians have very little help in the whole area of worship. Also essential Christian books read on to tapes, which would be of enormous benefit to the illiterate. Recordings of the Scriptures would also be valuable in areas where the written word is not easily available.

Through Derek Prince Ministries we have sent 140 dub master tapes in Mandarin of the *'Living Sacrifice'* programme into China — and also into courier centres like Singapore. There another precious colleague, Derrick Jacob, faithfully provides the materials to be carried into China by Christian business men and others who can hand them on to believers within China. In time — and that is a scarce commodity in China ministries — we will also produce more of Derek Prince's material

125

in tape form.

The provision of tapes is an excellent way of teaching and seeing leaders and others in China's church built up in the faith. Of course, they must have tape recorders for that, and provision of these machines is often a considerable blessing to these servants of God. Suitable machines can be purchased cheaply in Hong Kong and handed on through ministries with contacts in China.

Radio and tapes into China — a final word.

The way that God has used me in the radio and tape ministries into China has been a great encouragement to me. At times when I have found the English church scene difficult to cope with, it has been encouraging to know that the word that God spoke to me on a racecourse in the North of England has become the source of thousands upon thousands of people hearing the word of God regularly in China. When I feel discouraged in ministry (as most of us do from time to time — even Paul did), it helps to remember God's goodness in that way to me and through me.

I was recently in Singapore with Derek and Ruth Prince. Derek was speaking at a meeting where the congregation was made up of Christians of varied backgrounds — Caucasian, Chinese and other Asian groupings. He had asked me to share briefly at the start of the meeting about the Derek Prince Ministries involvement in China.

I poured out my heart. With apologies to those in the meeting who were not of Chinese extraction, I held up the China version of Derek's *"Foundation Series"* that has been prepared in Chinese for countries outside of China. I then pointed out that we were at that time very near to producing another Chinese version — one that will be especially prepared to be carried into China. It will be a cheaper, smaller and much less attractive version. No glossy cover with bright colours. One compact volume instead of seven.

Then I asked them which version excited them the most. There was the glossy Taiwan produced one that I held before them in my hand, designed for them and others to have the choice of buying — if they felt they needed it with all their other books. There was also the one that we were labouring to produce for China's hungry Christians, to give away to those who so hunger for such materials. Which one brought most joy to their hearts, I asked? I am sure that I do not need to give you the answer that I wanted!

Then Derek got up to speak. He began to say something that he had already shared with me on previous occasions. He said that if God took away all the ministry that he had, he would ask the Lord to take away one part of that ministry last. That last part would be the ministry that God had given him to China's growing and needy church.

Derek never actually finished what he wanted to say. He broke down and began to weep.

Derek was an Eton scholar, a Cambridge scholar and lecturer with enormous intellect. He has had a worldwide ministry for many years into many nations, which has been widely used and appreciated. But he was saying that he would give all of that away, if it really had to come to that before God, in order that he might serve China.

Need I say more?

CHAPTER 9

WILLING SERVANTS FOR CHINA

"Wang asked me one day to tell him more about the Bible. He listened to the Gospel over a period of time but found it difficult to fully trust in Christ. It was a real struggle for him. He was all alone in a city where he knew no other Christians. Later he told me: 'God is wonderful! What you told me is true!' He has been reading his Bible twice a day and found real encouragement. His friends are now asking about his faith and for Bibles. He added: 'There were many things I never understood in the Bible before I believed, but now it seems clear. Before, the only living Bible I was reading was you.'"

If we were talking together, as opposed to having to communicate through the pages of this book, I would want to ask you two questions about that exciting testimony. Who is "me"; and what is his or her relationship with Wang?

I doubt you would get the answer to my two questions right. The correct answer to the first is that "me" is someone from overseas who was working as a professional in China. The correct answer to the second is that Wang was someone with whom he or she came into contact, befriended and led to faith in Christ. This was because that foreigner lived a life in China that enabled this Chinese man to some extent to see Jesus.

There are opportunities today to live and work within China, in one of several ways. I want to share in this chapter about them. You will know by now, if you have got this far in the book, that I want to do more than share; I also want to challenge you to consider doing it, if your situation is in any way suitable!

For those who really want 'hands on' experience of China, and an opportunity to serve the Chinese people, there are avenues which can be pursued. There are many and varied opportunities for teaching in China. A more limited number of employment situations within China are open to Overseas Chinese or foreign Christians with technical, scientific, and professional skills of various kinds. Other situations are open for students in various disciplines, especially those who want to learn Chinese, as a whole or a part of their studies.

I shall divide these opportunities into three categories — *teachers; other professionals; and students*. But I need first to make some general comments that will apply to all three categories.

Christian professionals and students are needed who will go to serve the people of China with integrity. The servant attitude is of utmost importance, as is the quality of their lifestyle. They will be expected to share their skills and expertise without being patronising or superior, or to fit into their study environment without constant negative comments about material conditions or endless bureaucracy. The difference between Christians and non-Christians is often clearly seen by the Chinese people themselves in our attitudes to these matters. As a result questions are asked. The qualities of truth, love, patience and compassion do not go unnoticed in such a society.

There are restrictions that all professionals and students working in China need to be aware of and adhere to:

1. They are not allowed to distribute literature on an open basis. To do so could quickly lead to expulsion from the country. It can also endanger other Christians, both foreign and local, and jeopardise other opportunities.

2. No open evangelism or preaching is allowed, although there will be opportunities that arise for personal witnessing on a one to one (or more) basis.

3. No church planting or involvement with local church activity would be tolerated by the authorities, or normally encouraged by the house churches. It is the era of the indigenous church in China, and we are there to serve in a hidden and sometimes unrewarded way. There are some few opportunities for teaching the word of God, as the Lord leads.

4. No open advertising or public leading of Bible study groups or direct small group teaching is permitted, although requests from individuals or families can lead to a sharing of the Scriptures. Small low-profile discipleship groups for key and trusted contacts may be possible, but should have a self-destruct mechanism built into them, so that the young believers can be fed into local churches.

People are allowed in professional capacities into the country on the understanding that they are there to do a professional job. The authorities are sometimes very watchful of contacts that are made by foreigners and of their movements.

Having said all this, there is a deep spiritual hunger among the people, and it is relatively easy to get into witnessing situations with them through personal conversation in a variety of ways. Professionals often have contact with fairly important Chinese officials and with future leaders. The quality of their lifestyle can often lead to opportunities to witness. With the Chinese

131

people, however, relationships are all important, and their openness increases as trust is built up.

There are two extremes to be avoided: paranoia about sharing Jesus at all, or spouting forth at every apparent opportunity in the belief that this is fulfilling the Great Commission. It is easy to create a negative environment for foreign teachers who follow after — even to get them expelled. It is also easy to get local believers into trouble. There is a time to speak and a time to keep silent, and it is important to know the difference.

Any professional who is willing to work within the above limitations, love the people he or she is serving, and show a real concern for them, will be used by God. But there must be an exercise of God-given discernment. China is no place for the headstrong, the self-opinionated or the insensitive. It is a place for those who are teachable and willing to be highly accountable to the other foreign or local Chinese believers around them. For those who are willing to share their lives with a people who have never had a chance to enjoy the privileges so many of us take for granted, a rich harvest field awaits. Working in China is more than just an opportunity to teach and broaden one's experience. Openings to share Christ with colleagues, students and friends will come to those who know how to give themselves unreservedly, and who consequently inspire trust. One Chinese educational director put it very succinctly when he said, "We want devoted teachers." That sentiment would apply equally to the other categories listed below.

The most important qualifications for this type of work are a call to China, with a desire and willingness to serve and to grow spiritually. Academic qualifications or business and technical skills and commitment are obviously essential. There is, however, no substitute for a servant heart and the right kind of attitude. Whatever profession a Christian practises in China, it must not be used as a guise or disguise. There must be a genuine desire to serve the people of China in their attempt to modernise their nation.

Training and preparation are obviously essential. An understanding of the Marxist approach to life is vital — some of the students whom teachers will serve will have, since birth, assumed that no thinking or educated person could possibly believe in God; they would take it for granted that Christianity is part of the superstition of the uneducated. Specific Christian skills are needed in one-to-one Bible study and other areas. The ability to walk with the Lord, through personal quiet times, facing loneliness and pressure, will demand discipline and a heart-hunger for God. The professional is extremely unlikely to have access to the Bible teaching and worship celebrations to which he may be accustomed!

i) Teachers in China

Perhaps the greatest opportunity at present to serve in China is for those who are able to go and teach for a year or two — or more — in any of the post-secondary educational institutions or industrial departments that have for a number of years now sought to attract such people. In order to raise educational standards and to train a new generation, China must have people with a command of English. Universities and colleges are looking for people from English-speaking countries who are willing to come and help them in this task.

At present there are over 1,000 universities and colleges with nearly 2 million undergraduates and 100,000 graduate students. Christian teachers can make an impact upon the brightest minds of a fast developing land. Some teachers have led seeking students to Christ, and others, by their lifestyle and example, have made a noticeable impact.

Some universities have amazingly preferred Christian foreign teachers to non-Christian ones. This unlikely phenomenon is derived from the discernible difference in lifestyle between Christians and non-religious teachers living in China. Some Western teachers have brought

133

with them elements of our Western lifestyle that are unacceptable to the Chinese authorities — immorality, especially with their own students, alcohol problems and a generally negative and hostile attitude to the school authorities. In one of China's largest cities, applicants for teaching posts from abroad are automatically rejected if they state that they have no religion. The door is wide open for Christian teachers to find a job in China. It has also to be said that some unbelievers, on the other hand, show a commitment that should challenge many qualified believers in the West who are reluctant to surrender their "comfort zones".

In their teaching sphere they will be meeting sometimes with China's future leaders on various levels, and probably spending up to 20 weeks or more with the same group of students on an almost daily basis. They have a chance to gain the respect of these students through their conscientiousness, the quality of their teaching and their caring attitude. This will often lead to admiration for their moral lifestyle and eventually, as they unconsciously share their values and ideals, questions will be asked by the students about their beliefs. These may arise in private conversation, or in appropriate situations in the classroom, depending on the freedom of expression allowed by the particular institution. For Christian teachers this is a golden opportunity to attract people to the Lord Jesus and, in some cases, make an indelible impression that may have eternal significance.

Various groups can supply teachers with materials that will help them to explain the meaning of festivals like Christmas and Easter to the Chinese students. Classes have been known to ask openly what these festivals mean, and a carefully presented answer can be a powerful evangelistic tool.

Teachers of many disciplines are needed. In some situations it is preferable to be able to teach in Chinese, but those are a minority. Some of the sponsoring organisations take a firm stand on this matter, and recommend a one to two year spell in language study at one of China's universities that is equipped for such foreigners. Opinions differ here, and it will in part depend on the length of time the teacher intends to spend in China. The longer the commitment, the more the value in studying this great language. Mandarin Chinese, by the way, is the one to learn, unless you have a specific calling and desire to work with a minority people. Even then, some basics in Mandarin would be useful first, because the language of education and government of all China is Mandarin.

British people often make the mistake of thinking that Cantonese is widely used in China, because so many of the "Chinese takeaways" use it in the UK. Cantonese is a local dialect of the province that is next to Hong Kong, and is as relevant to most of China as French is to the average Englishman! It is usually a major advantage to speak Mandarin. Many teachers arrange for a willing, friendly Chinese person to give them some instruction in their spare time if they do not want to enter into full-time study.

Teaching in China calls for people of character and spiritual maturity. Applicants have to go through a fairly rigorous selection procedure as they must satisfy the standards of physical health, emotional stability and personal discipline called for by the demands that will be placed upon them in a different work environment and culture. It is very important that applicants are able to adjust to the cultural differences, and are willing to make a significant contribution to the academic and social aspects of life of an academic institution in China.

As far as qualifications are concerned, a university degree or teaching diploma and qualification in teaching English as a foreign or second language are normally acceptable. Obviously, even higher qualifications make the task of finding a suitable post that much easier, and the salaries may be higher. There are usually two different levels of grading of foreigners — foreign expert and foreign teacher. Pay and conditions differ accordingly.

It is sometimes possible to obtain jobs for people without these qualifications. This is especially so when it is clear that natural ability and potential will enable the teacher to handle the challenge of a classroom full of Chinese students. Some have gone out in faith — hopefully having first shared the matter with their local church leadership before they went — and have found that being in the right place at the right time caused the door they were looking for to open.

It is important to remember that China is a third world nation, and luxuries that are taken for granted in developed nations will be scarce, if they exist at all. Most teachers are paid enough to support themselves in China. Additional funds will be required for some teachers to cover travel costs as well as orientation and vacation periods spent in Hong Kong or home countries.

The ages of teachers range from graduates in their early twenties, to retired men and women in their sixties. Opportunities for married couples with children are more limited, especially for those with children of school age, but are usually available for those who are prepared to face the added pressures.

The actual task in the classroom varies considerably from one place to another. Foreigners could be asked to help in conversational skills, listening comprehension, writing, reading, English and American literature and Western culture. It is vital that the teacher can generate interest and enthusiasm in the subject. A lively approach is required, as well as consistent attention to developing the students' abilities in various language skills.

Some Chinese students expect their foreign teacher to be an authority on the Bible, because to them it is an important piece of English literature which has had considerable influence on Western thinking. It is, therefore, possible to share about Jesus within the classroom situation as long as one is creative and uses wisdom and discernment.

There are various approaches that may be taken by those interested in proceeding along the path of teaching in China. Firstly, short-term opportunities are arranged in China by some groups every year in different specialities — computers, languages etc. They are usually of around six weeks duration and include one week in Hong Kong and several weeks travelling in China. CCSM can help to put folk in touch with such groups.

Secondly, a larger step would involve an initial contract of one year for teaching, renewable by agreement by both sides at the end of that period.

Thirdly, a long-term commitment of at least five years might be possible. Two years of this would be spent in intensive language study and the other three working somewhere in China. The pay is low — but so is the cost of living.

Fourthly, for others the first step might be a short visit to China, if finances permit, to get the feel of the place. This is certainly advisable for someone who is thinking of a long-term commitment.

Teachers are normally placed in teams to provide support, care and fellowship, which are all very important in China. New teachers are normally placed in a situation where other colleagues are working either in the same college, or at the very least, in the same city.

There are a number of most reputable organisations that have been set up with the specific aim of locating the opportunities within China and then recruiting qualified Christians to take them. The shame is that there are usually more openings and requests for teachers than there are qualified Christians willing to take them. Such organisations establish relationships with national, provincial or local educational authorities, who may well know that they are Christian-based foundations, and yet still accept — sometimes gladly — the kind of quality

137

teachers they provide.

My own feeling is that in the majority of cases it is wisest to go out with such a foundation or organisation behind you. One important reason is that the Chinese educational authorities, who are usually working under very limited budgets, may try and extract unreasonably long hours of service from foreigners. This is not malice — it is just an effort to get as much as they can out of you. An organisation behind you that can negotiate a contract that is reasonable, as well as helping in the matter of living conditions, can be a great blessing.

Another reason for going via an organisation is that it is not easy to live and keep spiritually on top in a culture that is so different. There is the sometimes hostile Marxist atmosphere — you may wake up to patriotic songs blaring at you (that is not very conducive to exalted quiet times). You may also grow weary of being watched, with letters being opened, visitors noted, and sometimes unusually direct questions being asked. Your room may be bugged. Then there is the obvious matter of living in another country and culture — they eat different food, live in different ways and climates. I can remember early in my Taiwan days standing still outside a public building in a large crowd and finding it hard to stay calm when people kept bumping into me in a very un-Western way. An English relative reacted with astonishment at the loud belch which a Chinese Christian friend allowed herself to make after a good meal. What is socially unacceptable for one culture may be a point of appreciation for another. In such circumstances some pastoral resource in Hong Kong or elsewhere can prove very helpful.

Such organisations usually provide orientation courses before the prospective teacher enters China, and ongoing help in terms of adjustment and spiritual encouragement. In really bad moments, a phone call to a committed friend in Hong Kong or elsewhere does help!

Chinese Church Support Ministries aims to serve by putting Christians who are suitably qualified in touch with such organisations and foundations. We can advise as to how to proceed in the early days. Write to us if that would be helpful.

ii) Other professionals in China.

The opportunities for other professionals are much more limited in terms of scope. Some provide more contact with the Chinese people than others. Somebody working in the Diplomatic Corps, for example, would often have fairly limited contact with Chinese people. Journalists may have more contact, but their movements and contacts may at times be closely observed. Employees of large companies who conduct trade with China would have greater contact through business dealings with government representatives. They may also have the chance to befriend Chinese opposite numbers or those working in their offices. Relationships will normally remain fairly formal and distant, however, unless contact can be made on an informal basis outside of normal working hours.

There are vacancies for professionals in other fields, albeit somewhat limited. They include:

– Commerce. Types of Business Management and Training.

– Science and Technology. Scientists as teachers, researchers etc. Engineers of all kinds.

– Urban Development.

– Medicine. Usually fairly highly qualified medics are needed, although it may be possible to be part of a team doing short-term work in the country, including brief lecture tours.

– Arts. Opportunities for highly qualified musicians, artists, even fashion designers to visit and lecture in China.

For those with special abilities and economic backing, the possibility of opening a joint venture or some other kind of business exists. Labour is cheap and can be trained. There are many difficulties along this road, but it remains an exciting one. Some have already seen success in business and production in this area.

iii) Students in China.

Foreign students who study in a Chinese institution have some of the best opportunities to befriend the Chinese. However, situations differ widely in terms of friendship potential and access to spend time with Chinese fellow students. Sometimes that will depend on the policy enforced by the local authorities in the school concerned. At other times it may depend on the national policy at any given time. There are times (such as after the Tiananmen Square massacre) when Chinese are expressly warned not to have any contact with foreigners. They may be arrested if they do. Thus in certain situations it is possible to find oneself a little isolated from the Chinese students. That is a good reason for doing, if that is possible, what Jesus told His first disciples to do — to enter into a strange place two by two and not one by one.

But generally speaking those restrictions are much less true of the student category than they are of the other two above. Students are students — they have a way of befriending one another. Chinese students are generally of high quality and possessed of a desire to learn, a fact which makes the foreigner in their midst a source of untapped knowledge and potential best released through friendship.

For the foreigner it is important that he enter into genuine friendships with such people, rather than simply seek to "convert" them. Harm can be done in the long run when "friends" who do not respond to our agenda are dropped suddenly in favour of other more hopeful targets. Friendship is a vital and traditional quality in China. It is to be treasured. That is even more so after so much that has happened in recent years. There are wonderful opportunities to make lasting friendships and trusting relationships.

★★★★★★★★★★★★★★★★

The decisions reached after the October, 1987, 13th Party Congress had suggested that the present liberalisation policies would continue in China. It seemed that the leaders were firmly set on continuing to push for reform. They seemed determined to take China forward and make up some of the lost ground of the last few decades. China was, therefore, open to foreign Christians who might pray and consider taking jobs or studying in China to help in this process.

The events of the Tiananmen massacre, with the reversion to the more hardline Stalinist Li Peng regime, means that these policies now clearly face a setback. At the time of writing, we just do not know. The most likely eventuality is that there will be short-term setbacks in the economic policies — a possibly tentative period for China's economy. But I believe that the mid-term to long-term prospects are good. It is likely that we will see a resumption of the pre-Tiananmen days and directions before too long. Nobody, at this point, knows the timescale. The fact is that Deng wanted economic but not political change. There is so far no indication that his desire for new economic policies has reversed itself.

The general consensus has been that the economic and other changes are already so widespread and so thorough going that a complete reversal of policy in China would be impossible. Yet recent events would suggest that gun barrels and tanks, together with 'information' media that can be used with no reference to facts at all, makes many things possible. No-one can say for sure. It is a matter that demands much prayer.

We cannot say what effect this will have on the demand for professionals to help in China's modernisation programme, nor for the opportunities that had opened up through exchange and other study programmes for university level students. But I believe that the challenge to spiritual warfare remains — indeed it is greater than ever before.

Many years ago, one of the first foreign Christians in China wrote home and issued a clear challenge: "Give up your small ambitions and come to China."

Not much has changed since then. For all of the three categories I have listed above — teachers, other professionals and students — China offers fascinating, wide and challenging prospects. They are the more challenging when we consider the nature of the "small ambitions" that consume so many believers in the materialist West today. Are our ambitions really that important in the face of China's call to us today — and in the face of the price that Jesus paid for us and for one billion Chinese on the cross?

CHAPTER 10

STRANGERS IN OUR LAND

I was in England, not China, when I talked to Professor Zhou. He had been put in contact with me on a previous occasion while he was studying in England. Now we had the opportunity to share together face to face. We talked of many things, enjoying friendship and fellowship together. It was nearly time to go our own ways. I suggested that we pray together. I led off in Mandarin, thanking the Lord for His work in brother Zhou's life, and asking His blessing on the days to come after he returned to China. Suddenly I found that I was interrupted. Brother Zhou was weeping. I did not have to ask why. I knew that he has very little fellowship in China —as an intellectual he faces real dangers if he were to be open about his faith. The opportunity to pray together in Chinese with a trusted brother in the Lord was clearly so unusual for him that it touched the deep wound of spiritual loneliness within him.

His story is interesting. He had heard about Christianity over the radio while he was in China —probably through the Far Eastern Broadcasting Company or though Trans World Radio. He had become fascinated by what he heard, and a hunger to know more about the Lord Jesus grew up within him. However, he knew that it was far too dangerous to make any moves in that direction in his situation in China. Intellectuals like him have suffered much over the years for any "deviation", and he did not dare do more than listen secretly to the Christian radio programmes beamed in from abroad.

Then he was given an opportunity to take a period of time abroad in England to do some research. He made up his mind that he would seek the truth about God in that freer environment. But his initial efforts in England proved futile. The churches that he went to nearest to where he was staying seemed dull and uninteresting. Their content seemed almost unrelated to the Christianity that he had heard about on the radio programmes back in China. Sadly, he did not find the relationship with God that he was looking for. He therefore gave up looking in churches for the answer to his need. He resorted to watching television, hoping that he might find the answer there.

Then one day a Christian lady came into contact with him. In fact she attended a social gathering of some kind, to which Professor Zhou had been invited. I believe that she was probably there to 'fish' for just such a prepared heart. After Zhou had shared his predicament, she invited him to attend a meeting in her church. God met with Professor Zhou there in that church meeting in a powerful way —so much that was said under the leading of the Holy Spirit there seemed to be directly addressed to him. Thus he came to faith in the Lord Jesus at last, accepting the finished work of the Lord Jesus on the cross, receiving Him as his personal Saviour.

During the rest of his time in England he took every opportunity to study the Bible. He knew that once he went back he would have little opportunity to do so, and that he must redeem the time in England. I do not think that he knew a single Christian back in China —though he rather suspected, given what he now understood about Jesus, that one or two friends might be Christians. After he went back he continued that lonely walk —hence the tears when we prayed together.

The lessons here are compelling. Firstly, a hungry Chinese scholar of real quality came to a Western nation looking for Jesus Christ, and yet was unable to find Him in the first churches to which he went. Of course that would not by any means be universally true. But the fact is that this man could not find Jesus in a Western country by himself, even though he was specifically looking for Him! He did not know where to go or how to begin.

Secondly, one Christian lady, sensitive to the leading of the Holy Spirit, became what Philip was to the Ethiopian government official in Acts 8:26-40, and what Paul was to the Philippian jailer in Acts 16:25-34. She cared and she listened to the Holy Spirit. By those simple steps she led a key person into an eternal and fruitful relationship with the Lord Jesus!

But I am not just recounting a story for its own sake, just to bless and thrill you. The fact is that some of you who read these pages could be used of the Lord in just the same way. You can do something if you have a burden to be involved personally with the Chinese, but do not however have the time, training or the finance to visit or work in China itself. You can take practical steps to serve the Lord and the Chinese. For some this is a way of reaching Chinese people without leaving their own country —and possibly even without moving from the comfort of their own home!

Since Deng Xiaoping initiated China's Open Door policy in 1978, as part of the Four Modernisation Programme, China has sent tens of thousands of scholars and students to more than seventy countries for specialised training. This elite group of people will be expected to return to China, after they have completed their training, to help in the country's drive towards modernisation. Huge numbers of them are studying in the United States, in Canada, in Australia and New Zealand, and in European countries such as Germany, France, and Great Britain.

There is a priceless opportunity for believers in Western or other countries who live within driving distance of universities and places of learning to reach out to them.

The Chinese scholars are divided into three main groups:

1. Senior scholars, usually professors or research scientists, sent by the government for one or two years training. They are not therefore normally working for a degree.

2. Younger graduates who normally have been involved in some form of government service or university teaching or research for at least two years. This requisite will vary according to the practices of the different Chinese universities in which they work. Sometimes they will have been cleared for their political reliability.

3. Scholars and students of all ages who have been privately sponsored.

To understand their situation, we need to put ourselves in their shoes. We need to try to understand what they are like and what they feel about us.

Firstly, they are in a strange and foreign country. Many of them are completely overwhelmed by what they see when they first arrive in a Western country. They face loneliness in a new country, far away from family and friends —many are married and have left husbands or wives and their child at home in China. Culture shock is a real problem. They are often confused by the lifestyle of the West, amazed at the amount of freedom people seem to have in every walk of life, yet shocked by our individualism and selfishness. But they are usually very keen to understand Western culture and will usually welcome any invitation to a home.

During the first few weeks they are especially in need

146

of help. They need friends who are prepared to take time out to show them around their immediate environment, in order to help them settle in as quickly as possible. Christian research or undergraduate students on university campuses and other places like that have especially good opportunities for service here.

They will be under a great deal of pressure to do well in their studies. They therefore desire to spend most of their time in study. That need should be respected. They should not be put under too much pressure to take part in an endless round of social activity. Apart from anything else, while they are adjusting to the new language, they will find it fairly difficult to keep up with their studies.

Secondly, they are often open to hospitality.

Christians in the host countries have a tremendous opportunity to introduce them to Christ. But I believe that the key to that is first to offer them genuine friendship, love and hospitality. Many of them love children and miss their own (often one child under China's one child per family policy). Remember that some may have left their child while he or she is only a few years old, missing a chance to see them grow that they will never have again. It is therefore therapeutic and a blessing to them to be in a family or home setting.

Thirdly, they often are not very well off.

The Chinese education budget is under great pressure. Thus especially government sponsored scholars (as opposed to privately sponsored ones) may not have much spare cash. That presents us with great opportunities to serve them by taking them out for the day to some local scenic place or national treasure, or to some museum or place of learning or interest. See if there are reasonable material needs with which you can help them.

By the way, the Chinese will almost always bring you a small gift when they come to eat at your house. It may be some candies, or pictures and cut-outs, or a silk

handkerchief or something like that. Their culture says
that they must do that. Express gratitude for it. Make
sure, if you go to eat in the place where they are living,
that you do the same. Nothing fancy —a teatowel, some
small thing of local interest or whatever.

Fourthly, they are not all the same.

The Cultural Revolution stereotype must be put aside.
They are as different in interests, political bias, spiritual
hunger and food tastes as the people of our countries
are.

Very often one or more are assigned to report to
Embassy officials about the activities of their fellow
scholars. Do not be surprised if they do not wish to talk
to you on spiritual or other personal matters whilst in
the presence of others. It may even happen that, having
been vocal before, they clam up suddenly. They may be
nervous about someone else in the room. Remember that
the Chinese Embassy in certain places actually took
covert videos of the demonstrations outside of China
after the Tiananmen massacre, subsequently phoning
and warning some of the scholars in these countries
about future involvement in any of that kind of activity.
You may even find that some in the same department
do not talk to each other at any real level. Just accept
that there is much you do not understand, and leave it
at that. It is far better to invite one or two home than a
large group, as they will be more likely to talk freely in
small numbers.

Some are clearly hardline party members; some even
now believe that China needs to revert to the Mao days,
if not the Cultural Revolution days. That may not be
what you think — it may simply be that they do not
know what happened, because there was as total a
government blackout of the truth then as there was after
the events of June 1989.

Some are seeking answers and are open to Christianity.
Others are not. Most are unused to the immoral and
decadent atmosphere on Western campuses, though a

148

few seem to get sucked into that. Accept that each is different.

It is thus important to be sensitive to the different types of scholars. A few may be committed Communists, but many, in spite of their Marxist training, may be seeking answers to the meaning of life. They may be very open to hearing about Christianity. A love for them and the ability to make friends with them is essential, as is a sense of humility and a genuine desire to understand the background from which they have come.

Some tips for the nervous beginner!
There is only one key. Learn to listen to them. Remember that they are by culture quite, quite different from many Westerners —they do not always say what they think, and even when they do, they may not be quick to say it. Give them space, accept them for what they are, and love them with the love of the Lord Jesus. This kind of friendship evangelism provides a good opportunity to demonstrate the love of God. It is also a chance to influence people who might well be important leaders when they return to China.

There are no invariable rules of witnessing in such situations, but there are one or two things that might help. Stereotyped techniques of evangelism will not necessarily be very helpful. As mentioned in the previous chapter, a relationship of trust is all-important to the Chinese people. This will have to be established first through practical demonstrations of the love of God.

Chinese scholars will often accept invitations to Christian festivals or weddings, but it is important to guard them against foolish questions of well-meaning people. They certainly should not be exposed to people who are likely to launch headlong into an attack on Communism! It is wise not to criticise Communist party politics or the present leadership of China. This could cause embarrassment and estrangement. You are unlikely to discover easily their political sentiments unless you know the signs. Even Party members would be unlikely to admit that to you. The subject of politics is then better given a wide birth.

A good working knowledge of the Bible would certainly not go amiss, as well as the ability to think through some of the questions that a scholar from a Marxist background might ask. The sort of questions posed might be: What is truth? Is it relative or absolute? Can the Party define truth and change it? Can yesterday's truth become today's lie? What is human nature? Can it be changed? Is it really possible to produce a society of selfless individuals? What value has the individual? Is Christianity a superstition to deceive people? Does Christianity have a solid historical background? Can you give evidence for the death and resurrection of Christ? Is a belief in any form of miracles not to be seen as a superstition and therefore to be rejected in this modern scientific age?

It is always best to be as prepared as possible and to think through some of these issues. They may well be vital questions which will be of the utmost importance to the scholars who bring them up.

It is quite possible that they will be embarrassed if, having been invited to a home, they then find that the entertainment is too extravagant for their taste. The need for sensitivity in this area cannot be over-emphasised.

Remember as well that they do like different foods from us. Our best intentioned efforts to honour them may not be well appreciated. An American friend told me how he had known of a Chinese scholar who was invited to a thanksgiving meal in the States. Replete with turkey and all the trimmings and whatever else he had been offered, he eventually returned to his lodgings. There he promptly cooked some rice and ate it —he felt the need of something that to him was a real meal! If you are really honoured, after they get to know you they may even offer to cook real (Chinese) food for you in your own home!

They should be allowed to bring up the subject of

religion themselves. It is always far better to answer their questions than to try and force the conversation down that road. There are bound to be opportunities to discuss Christianity when talking about life in the West. The matter will almost certainly arise naturally. There is no need to try and force the pace.

God's work and man's need

When all is said and done —relax! You do not need to speak Chinese —they would not be in your country if they could not speak at least some of your language —though if you have a heavy dialect, you might like to slow down when you speak! You do not need to be an expert on Sino-European or Sino-American relationships, or to be able to pronounce the name of any Chinese leader, or to be able to pick up ten peanuts in 20 seconds with chopsticks in your left hand. All you need to know is a secret that I have found over the years —that the Chinese are (with, of course, some notable exceptions) some of the most honourable, excellent and quality people on the face of the earth. The privilege may well be yours —and the enjoyment as well.

But then you might say that I am biased!

Remember that it is the Holy Spirit's job to bring such scholars and students to an awareness of their need of Christ. The most important and effective task that we can do is to pray for them regularly and undergird all that we do with this powerful weapon. So love them and go for it!

At the time of writing, the situation is especially sensitive for many of them. They have seen the recent events in China carried daily on Western news footage, and are horrified at the carnage and murder of their fellow students and scholars. Some of them are very frightened of what lies ahead. They fear that the Chinese Embassy could call them back, saying that their funding has been terminated. They do not know what would happen if they had to return to China. Some have spoken

151

to me of lying awake at night, unable to sleep in fear. Some foreign governments, seeing the seriousness of their situation, have offered extensions to visas if required. It is a time of fear and darkness for them. Many desire to extend their stay in foreign countries until they can understand what will happen in China in the months and years to come.

I pray that the situation may have changed by the time that you read this. It is a time of uncertainty for them. It is a challenge for special concern —and loving action —from us.

CHAPTER 11

JOURNEY OF A LIFETIME

I fell into conversation with a young Chinese on a Beijing street a few years ago. He turned out to be a student at one of the leading universities in the city. We found we had much common ground. I had taught for several years at Taiwan University, the leading University on the Island. I was therefore interested to meet with this Mainland Chinese equivalent of the hundreds of Chinese students that I had taught and known in Taiwan. He, for his part, was probably in the same way interested by the comparison.

The next day, at his invitation, I visited his university. It was a very exciting time for me. Two main memories stick in my mind. The first was one of his friends declaring to me in a loud clear voice at a public bus stop how much of a waste of time he considered their compulsory political education to be. I was not happy with that, as it was neither an appropriate time nor subject for me to be discussing with him. But it was a sign of the times — even then in the early eighties.

The second main memory is more important. He took me into his very primitive (by our non-Chinese

153

standards) dormitory. We sipped hot chocolate and chatted. In the middle of a general conversation, one of the students looked at me and asked me in Chinese, without any preliminaries whatsoever, how he could find God!

I was in a quandary. I had a lot of literature with me back at the hotel. I did not want to jeopardise the delivery of that vital material. I really did not know if it was a genuine question — or a trap. So, regretfully, I decided to let it pass.

However I did take the address of the student I had met on the street. Later, after I had returned to England, I shared the incident with a Christian businessman who at that time travelled frequently into China. I arranged for him to take a Bible into China on his next trip addressed to my student friend. That at least would be a way of helping to answer the question that the other student had asked.

Imagine my surprise when, a few months later, the Christian businessman contacted me with the account of what had happened. He had posted the Bible from a hotel post office, though not from the actual hotel in which he was staying at the time. However my student friend tracked him down in his hotel and came to him. "Do you", the student asked, "have any more Bibles? You see, a third of our university is seeking for God!"

Later the two of them even worked together to put Christian literature into the English section of one of the libraries at that particular university!

Exciting opportunities like that exist for those who feel that it is right to use their finances and their vacations for something more challenging and fulfilling than a few lazy days on a beach somewhere. There is the opportunity to see God lead in unusual ways — to see something of His sovereignty in that great land.

I long that many Christians should get out of their little holy huddles, out of their over-fed and under-exercised environments, and see the rest of the world as it really is. It amazes me how blind so many of us are to the real world — with so many hungering to hear the Gospel just once and with so many urgently needing just a tenth of the books, tapes and meetings that we have.

I often think that if the average church could be transported to a city street in Shanghai and just see that mass of Chinese humanity (most of whom may never have heard the Gospel), it would have to do something to stir us up. Or if the average church could cram into the little rooms where Wang Mingdao and others live, in order to hear them share about their experience of the Lord Jesus, it surely would help us to wake up to the real world outside.

It is not just that the Christian world has changed. Of course it has changed — Patrick Johnstone estimates that in 1900 about 91 percent of all born again Christians were in the West, and only 9 percent in all the other countries. Now about 60 percent of them live outside of the West. We are the minority now. But it is more than that kind of change. These other lands have a different set of priorities — like the leader who wrote to me from his Asian country and said that he would be planting 40 churches in his country next year, and therefore probably would not have time to attend a British conference at which he was invited to speak. They have a different spirituality, a different vision, a different expectation. We need to learn from them, especially from our brethren in China!

So I do long for many believers to break out, travel overseas and see what I and others have seen — especially about those one billion souls in China alone. I believe that it would change us, and act as a mirror to let us see how self-centred is so much of what we live for and expect as our rights.

Yet I do have a problem with that. The problem is that trips to China are expensive. I would rather see that money go into the China ministries that I have mentioned to be used in the Lord's work!

Perhaps a middle line is required then on this matter of tourist trips to China. An obvious statement would be that we only go if we feel that the Lord is really leading us. Another way of putting it would be this — do we go to get or to give, to indulge ourselves in China's comfortable hotels and classic tourist sights, or to serve the people of China in whatever way God may lead?

What do I mean by service — what can be done by a tourist to China?

Let me suggest three basic alternative holiday packages:

i) The normal holiday package with two variations.

a) *The typical package tour.* This is suitable for Christians who feel that they would like to visit China without hassle as tourists. These trips can be arranged in a variety of ways, either in the home country or in Hong Kong. On this type of trip everything is taken care of for you — where you stay, how you travel, what and whom you see. It is most suitable for those who have little experience in travel and who would be intimidated by having to make their own arrangements in a strange country.

b) *The individual visa tour.* This would ideally be undertaken with one or two other Christian friends. On this type of trip you are very much on your own. You must make your own arrangements to travel in and out. That can be a walk of faith, as many times you cannot make advance bookings — but you may find that all flights out to Hong Kong from where you are fully booked (and it may be two days on a train!). I once needed to get myself and two companions out of Shanghai, only to be told that there were no flights for ten days. But it is a good opportunity to hear God and see Him provide — as we found on that occasion! On the "private visa", you are on your own for hotels and meals as well.

The advantage of the "private visa" over the tour package lies in the fact that your time is your own.

Within the permitted cities you may go when and where you wish. You do not need to be with a group going round a carpet factory — unless you want to be! It is therefore easier to make chance or deliberate acquaintances. It may have its moments, however, as when on one occasion, on a 36 hour train journey, almost everyone in the compartment in which I was travelling started to get off the train at a station in the middle of nowhere. I was able to ask in Chinese what was happening. I was told that this was the only way to get to the buffet car, because the rest of the train was so full. We needed to walk down the platform and climb into the other carriage, and then do the same thing in reverse at the next station. It could have been very unsettling if I had not been able to ask why we were being deserted by all and sundry miles from the train's destination!

As far as trains go, there are three classes (yes, in Communist China there are classes). Soft sleeper (very comfortable and more expensive, with only four people per carriage); hard sleeper (it is hard, but not unreasonably so, and there are many people to talk to, with whom you may be travelling for up to 36 hours); and hard seat (to be avoided for long overnight journeys by all but the real pioneers. I do know one brother who travelled for about ninety hours like that). I recommend the hard sleeper. Be friendly and get to know the people around you.

In China itself, the people are basically friendly to foreigners. Foreign visitors are always welcome to attend Sunday meetings held in a TSPM church and meetings can be arranged with church pastors. It is very unlikely, however, that tourists can visit house churches. Many meet in secret and a visit could cause them great difficulty and even considerable danger.

Only if a definite invitation is received or a definite purpose authorised should a foreign visitor go to a Chinese Christian's home. Some Christians are free to receive foreign visitors, but they must take the initiative in the situation. It is important to be sure that the visit will not cause the hosts any problems with the authorities. Remember that you may be followed, though you would never know that, and the person that you visit might be the one to get into trouble.

China does not allow open evangelism, street corner preaching or distribution of religious literature. But some Chinese are inquisitive or searching. They may ask a question of a foreigner on the street or during a chance encounter. Others simply do not wish to know. Others again are not willing to take any risks. It is often a question of walking each day in a position of availability to the Holy Spirit. He can pick hungry hearts for you — after all, He has a billion from which to choose.

It may be possible to get in touch with Christians from abroad who are working in China. They should be contacted ahead of time, if at all possible. It should be remembered that all mail may be censored and telephone calls may be recorded. The subjects of Bibles or other sensitive issues should never be mentioned in letters, nor should there be any reference to missionary work or Christian witness in any communication. You should not mention names, especially those of Chinese Christians. That kind of reference could well be intercepted by the authorities and could cause real problems for the person who is working in China.

I would encourage those who go into China as tourists in either category I have mentioned in this section to take Bibles and other materials into China. The best way is to get them in Hong Kong from groups like Revival Christian church, Open Doors, YWAM, Christian Communications Ltd and others. They will also advise regarding those to whom you should give them. Even if you have no known contacts to whom to give them, you can look to the Lord to lead you. There are no hard and fast rules about how much material to take in. Let the Lord be your wisdom in that.

ii) The adventure package.

As well as the two kinds of normal holiday package, this third possibility exists for those who are younger, or more bold by natural or spiritual inclination. It is also for those who have some time to spare – perhaps as a student or between jobs.

There is a real need for Christians who would be willing to go to Hong Kong for a couple of weeks, or even a few months, to carry literature and Bibles over the border into China. There are groups which specialise in this – such as Revival Christian Church. Cheap (and basic) accommodation can be recommended in Hong Kong, advice and help given for visas, literature provided, teams set up and directed. They are a most unusual and committed group of believers. This type of ministry will involve travelling in and out of China many times. You will have the opportunity to work with Christians from different countries with very different backgrounds.

Another adventure package possibility to be considered is that of taking a summer break to work in exchange camps, either learning Chinese, teaching English or being involved in specialised areas such as computers.

Chinese Church Support Ministries can help put you in touch with groups who specialise in these different areas of ministry to China. But there is one factor to note here – CCSM does not offer any travel service facilities!

As well as being able to give something to China, you should expect to gain much. Many who have travelled to China have found it to be a life-changing experience. At the very least, they have come away with a better understanding of how to pray for the needs of that fascinating country. Pray about it – it could change your life!

CHAPTER 12

WHY SHOULD WE?

In the previous chapters I have shared my heart with you about some of the varied ministries for China in which Chinese Church Support Ministries and many other ministries (but by no means enough of them) are involved today. But there is a further question which I now need to address in this chapter.

Why, some may say, give our energies and resources to China when we have heard that there is revival there already? Are there not, according to some reports, 50 million believers there today? Why not turn to lands where there is no revival, for surely they are much more in need of our attention.

I do understand something of the needs of other nations. I have travelled and ministered in some of them myself — including many of the Eastern European nations. I fully endorse any legitimate missionary efforts for any nation in the world today. We want more for every nation, not less! I am not seeking to be negative about any missionary outreach to any nation in the world. If I were to do so, I would be at enmity with my my Lord Jesus, Who said that we were to "go and make disciples of all nations" (Matt 28:19). I am simply seeking to be particularly positive about one nation — China!

I could argue from the facts. Between one quarter and one fifth of the world's population live in that one nation. Suppose we drew a missionary map by the number of people in each country, rather than by the size of the land. That would put a very strong case for China. Someone has said that one person in every three in the world of those who do not know Jesus lives in China today. I do not know if that figure is correct — but it cannot be too far out!

I believe the situation in China is particularly in need of our prayer and resources for several reasons. I am going to discuss three of them in this chapter.

1. The first reason concerns the need to make correct spiritual investment.

When we see the Spirit of God moving in a country, we must invest our time, energy and resources there. There is a revival happening in China that is causing the church of Christ to grow at a rate that is probably unprecedented in the two thousand years of its history. This is a situation that demands our investment.

Patrick Johnstone, the director of research for WEC International, makes some classic observations about China in his book *"Operation World"*. Speaking of the "manifest bankruptcy of human ideologies in China", he observes that "there may be more Christians than Communist party members"! Some towns and villages "have a Christian majority" — in a land that has been in the grip of atheistic Marxism for 40 years. "Never in history", Johnstone records, "have so many been converted over such a short time. Between 1977 and 1984 many millions have come to faith in Christ". In fact Dennis Balcombe has discovered that the current revival in one area of central China only began at the end of that period mentioned by Johnstone — in the 1983 period of persecution and repression.

We are seeing in China a move of God of unparalleled depth.

David Wang, Executive Vice-President of Asian Outreach, tells the story of a visit he made to a pastor in November 1988. The pastor lived in a mountainous area of China and had been imprisoned for almost twenty-three years. Before he was sentenced by the authorities, there were 170 believers in the whole of the county where he lived.

In 1986 he was finally released, and when he came home he was desperate to find out what had happened to the Christians he had left behind. All of the time in prison he had been praying for them, concerned that, in the words of Scripture, without a shepherd the sheep would be scattered.

He asked his son how things were in the church, to which his son replied, "Father, when you were sent to prison, there were 170 believers, now there are 5,000!"

The pastor could hardly believe his ears — in fact he found it very difficult to accept what his son told him. Consequently he carried out a survey of the whole county, checking meticulously how many believers there were. His results proved it — there were indeed 5,000.

David Wang relates how amazed he himself was at this report, and was even slightly skeptical. "But that is not all," the pastor continued, "that was two and a half years ago. Today we have 56,000 believers!"

"But how many people are there in this county?" asked David. "60,000", was the reply.

David left the pastor's home in a slight state of shock. In his heart he wanted to believe what he had heard, but his intellect kept telling him that such a thing was not possible. Leaving the mountainous area, he went to a nearby town to spend some time with the pastor of the Three Self church. He wanted to question him about what the old pastor had claimed, and knowing that the

Three Self pastor was appointed by the authorities, he would probably understate the case by far, perhaps enabling David to gain a more balanced and correct view of the situation.

David told the Three Self preacher what the old pastor had said. "Oh yes," the preacher exclaimed before David had hardly had time to get the words out of his mouth, "it is wonderful what God is doing. But do you know what has happened in our church?"

He then related the story of a peasant woman, living way out in the countryside, who had developed a large growth on the side of her body. She had watched it grow over a short period from the size of a pea, to that of a basketball. In desperation she had travelled to the town, seeking help from any doctor who was willing to listen to her. Very few did, even though she begged them on her knees. One gave her some attention, but he had only one recommendation to make: "Cut it! If you live, you live. If you die, you die."

Completely desolate, the woman stumbled around the town, not knowing where to turn for help. As she passed a particular side road, memories of fifty years earlier suddenly flashed through her mind. As a young girl she had come to town and walked past the same road. She remembered that she had heard music coming from a particular building, and then someone had come out of the building and offered her a candy bar. When she unwrapped it, there was a piece of paper inside, upon which was written the basic facts of the gospel, and how Jesus had come to save mankind.

As these pictures came to the old peasant woman again, she rushed to the building, and banged loudly and continuously on the door. The Three Self pastor who was relating the story was the one to open the door to her. "Jesus help me. Jesus help me," was all she would say.

The pastor took her in, calmed her down, and got her to tell him what was troubling her. When she had finished, he prayed for her, and sent her on her way. On the journey home the woman witnessed a miracle. Slowly, but surely, the growth decreased in size, until, by the time she reached her village, it had completely disappeared.

A few days later there was more banging on the door of the church building in the town. When the pastor opened the door, the old woman was there again with nine members of her family. They had all seen what God had done for her, and wanted to become Christians.

A few weeks later, fifteen bullocks pulling fifteen carts arrived in the courtyard of the church building. They were piled high with people and all kinds of superstitious charms. A large number of the villagers had come wanting to know Jesus, and to burn all their occult charms. There was a huge bonfire in the courtyard as the instruments of darkness were reduced to ashes. "Within a very short space of time," the pastor told David, "I baptised 199 people. Two weeks later I baptised 199 more. Then two weeks after that I baptised another 199."

"That is quite remarkable," David replied. "But tell me something. Why exactly 199 each time." "Oh that's simple," the pastor answered with a smile, "if I had baptised 200, I would have had to inform the authorities!"

With such amazing experiences, dramatic conversions, and explosive growth, we must invest with everything that we have, while the Holy Spirit is so clearly moving in China. We should be taking the view that we need to win as many people for the Lord as we can.

Our goal should be to pray and sow in the word of God. We need to flood in the word of God while we have the opportunity. China may remain open — and become even more open. On the other hand, it could close its doors completely again. But now, at this moment, there is a partly open door, and we must take full advantage of the time God has given to us.

There is an incredible revival taking place in China. In Henan province, where there is a remarkable work of the Holy Spirit, the growth of the church is even admitted by the authorities. Government officials a few years ago have reportedly stated that about 10% of the population of Kaifeng (total population 640,000) are Christians, compared with 1% in 1949.

The growth has not been confined to Henan, however. The gospel has spread to virtually every province of China, and some have seen spectacular growth.

One pastor shared that he believed there could be as many as 5 million believers in Zhejiang province alone. In 1986, a pastor told an overseas visitor that were close to 1 million believers in Jiangsu province, and that there was also a group of 80 independent house churches in Shanghai where the membership ranged from 90 — 350 people. Another report spoke of 1,000 house churches still active in the city.

In Qinghai province, an area notorious for its labour camps, there has been a remarkable multiplication in the number of Christians. It is one of China's largest provinces, but has a population of only 4 million, traditionally inhabited by Tibetans, but now also by the Han Chinese, who are now in the majority, and the Hui, who are Muslims. In 1950 there were only 120 known Christians. Today a conservative estimate puts the number at 2,100. The main church in Xining holds 400 people, but there are reckoned to be at least 1,500 Christians in the city. Over the last two years 1,200 have been baptised, with at least another 500 waiting.

Xinjiang province is a strong Muslim area. Before 1949 there were only a few hundred believers in the whole province. Now it is now estimated the figure could be as high as 10,000. It is even reported that there are thriving house churches in the far west of the province, on the Sino-Soviet border.

The gospel has also penetrated the tribal people, such as the Lisu, Miao and Yi, of which there are large numbers in China. In the fifties, Lisu Christians suffered much for their faith, and many of them fled to Burma. A number of the pastors and church workers were sent to work in the mines, and the church appeared to be all but completely wiped out.

Recent reports tell a different story. In Yunnan province it is estimated that the majority of some 300,000 believers are from the Lisu. Lisu evangelists claim that every Lisu village now has a church and that half of this tribal people are Christians.

Luquan County in Yunnan has around 40,000 Christians, most of whom are from the Yi minority people, meeting in 300 churches and countless home meetings. When a new church is officially dedicated, it is not unusual to have 1,000 Christians present. In one part of this province, 95 percent of believers have became Christians since 1976.

In Heilongjiang, formerly known as Manchuria, there are strong churches among the Korean minority people who live just inside the Chinese border, close to North Korea. The TSPM has set up in many counties in this province, but elsewhere where this is not so there are also large numbers of people accepting Christ into their lives. In one county where the TSPM is not strong, they are seeing more people converted than anywhere else in the province. Two thirds of the villages have meeting points.

In Shandong province, aggressive evangelism has produced incredible results. A preacher visited a certain area where he found 200 believers. A few months later, a further six workers returned to the area to preach. As they did so, the Lord confirmed His word with healings and miracles and, as a result, 4,000 new converts were baptised in six days.

In another district a woman was saved as a result of listening to a radio broadcast She was also healed of an incurable disease. Her husband was not a Christian. She therefore prayed for him for two hours every day for three months. Eventually he was saved. Together they began to preach the gospel in a district near the Yellow River. As a result they have seen 3,000 people become Christians in two years.

On Hainan Island, off the south China coast, there is great growth in the TSPM churches, as well as the house churches. A TSPM pastor reported 10,000 believers in the church there, but their activities are very much controlled by the United Front Work Department. Other sources say that the number of house church Christians in one county in eastern Hainan Island has grown from 5,000 to 9,000.

In another area, an old pastor was released after many years in prison. He returned to his village, began preaching the gospel faithfully, and after only three months saw a church established and grow to 700 people. Much of the growth is as a result of such fearless and enthusiastic evangelism, coupled with an unusually powerful movement of the Holy Spirit.

Although the TSPM puts the number of Christians at 5 million for the whole of China, other sources consider that the figure of 50 million favoured by many Chinese observers may even be on the conservative side. The thrilling thing about all that is happening is that after nearly forty years of isolation, without missionaries, Bibles, church buildings, and many things considered to be so necessary for church life outside of China, the church in China has emerged, not just surviving by the skin of her teeth, but thriving, expanding and even exploding at an unbelievable rate. In the last seven or eight years the house churches have multiplied ten times over. The church in China now represents the largest body of believers in the world.

We do rejoice to see that the sovereign Holy Spirit, in His mercy, is investing in China. We need to follow His example. As He has moved across China, there have been signs and wonders, healings, miracles, the casting out of demons, angelic visitations and all kinds of supernatural interventions. As a result, conversions on a massive scale have taken place.

The response of God's people in China has played a significant part, as they have consistently engaged in evangelism, in spite of opposition and persecution. They have invested in the move of God. As the situation has eased in the country, so their witnessing has become even bolder and more aggressive. They have responded to the needs of a people disillusioned by Communism. After the death of Mao many people were left without purpose to life, and the Christians have begun to show in very clear ways where abundant life can be found.

Such a work of God requires our urgent support — our investment. We must invest our resources where they are most needed and will be best used at this moment in time. How much we need to learn from the world. Jesus said that the children of this world are wiser than the children of the Light (Luke 16:8). The businessman, the investment expert, were he to see the natural equivalent of what we are seeing spiritually in China, would invest in it at once. In terms of the kingdom of God, so should we!

That is why Chinese Church Support Ministries and other China ministries are so busy with that work. But we cannot do it alone. Others must help us, with prayer, with finance, with workers. Others must see the need to invest in China. The thousands of new churches require leaders who are trained in the word of God. Scores of letters from house church leaders reach Hong Kong begging, yes, literally begging for assistance of various kinds. They require help of various kinds and we outside of China have the resources with which to help.

2. My second reason for concentrating on China concerns the need to fight heresy.

As thrilling as the revival is in China, it has also brought to light a number of problems. During the Cultural Revolution all Bibles and Christian literature found by the fanatical Red Guards were confiscated and destroyed. Now that there is a slightly more relaxed approach, with the number of Christians growing at such a rate, there are nowhere near enough Bibles to give to new converts. In fact, one Bible shared between one hundred believers is closer to the norm, and in many places they are much more scarce.

The result of this lack of God's word is that heresies exist among some believers. In some cases bizarre sects spring up, which, because of their extremism in some form or other, only add fuel to the fire of the authorities, in their criticism of and opposition to the church.

Selwyn Hughes, in his recent excellent and incisive writing on revival in "Every Day With Jesus", has made some observations that are critical to our correct understanding of the situation in China. He points out that revival brings to the fore not only the spiritual side of man's nature, but also the baser and more carnal side. A commentator at the high point of the Methodist revival said: "When our soul came to taste the feasts of heaven, the flesh also insisted on having its share, and all the passions of nature aroused by grace were rioting tumultuously". Revival does not abolish at one fell swoop human carnality or the defects of our nature. Even at Pentecost there were those who lost their love and joy and slipped back into a wordly spirit. But that did not make the power any less real or genuine. Jonathan Edwards said that if the Corinthian church had been left to themselves, they would have torn themselves to pieces, even though the Holy Spirit was at work amongst them. If the New Testament church had to face that kind of problem, so does China today.

The balance of understanding of revival, according to Selwyn Hughes, is a critical but simple one. Revival does bring a powerful and potentially life changing touch through the sublime and joyous feelings that it brings. At the same time it is vital that we understand that this is not that which effectively changes the character of the believer. Such feelings cannot last, and no-one can live that way continuously. It is the teaching and pastoral ministry of the church that brings that deeper change. Sound teaching must be available to channel the high ecstasy and emotion seen in times of revival into productive purposes. Without that, revival can induce great spiritual pride. For example, young men may be carried away by pride after a high peak in their spiritual experience. William Williams said of one such: "He was a raw youth whom no-one would entrust to shepherd his sheep and is riding high in a boldness of spirit much superior to old ministers who have borne the burden and heat of the day". Do you not see that that may happen in China today?

So we need to heed the words of warning of men like Emyr Roberts. "The cultivation of Christian virtues, and the building of sound and sane Christian character, is the work, under the blessing of God, of the pastor and the teacher". Commentators have even said that the 1904 Welsh revival could have lasted longer and made an even greater spiritual impact if there had been more teachers and teaching resources to lead the people into the deeper things of God.

The application of that insightful teaching by Selwyn Hughes to China is only too obvious. We could print a whole book of glorious testimonies, and no doubt be richly blessed by them. Hopefully all of the above are accurate. But they may not mean much, or may not impact China as much as they could, if we do not invest in that second stage of taking into China the word of God, teaching ministries and materials of every suitable kind, as fast and as much as we can.

In some country areas there is evidence of Christianity being mixed with local folk-belief and Buddhism. Other sects are flourishing because of their powerful preaching and miracles, often going to excess in the realms of exorcism and healing.

Brother Andrew of 'Open Doors' related the story of

an itinerant evangelist who travelled the country faithfully preaching about Jesus, even though he had no Bible himself. On one of his journeys he fell into a narrow pit and was trapped, hanging upside down. Whatever he did, he could not free himself, and was firmly held by the sides of the pit, with only his feet protruding out of the top.

He began shouting for help, to no avail. He struggled to get free, but had no success. After about an hour of carrying on in this fashion, he remembered prayer. Just as he began to pray, someone else came along the road, saw his predicament, and helped him out of the pit.

He was naturally very grateful to the person concerned, and above all else to God for answering prayer. He explained his answer to prayer in the following way, however. "Earlier, my prayers were never answered so promptly, but when I prayed upside down, God answered immediately."

When he came to the next village on his itinerary, he explained what had happened to him. Out of this experience was born a new sect, which now numbers thousands of followers, who, when they meet together for prayer, stand on their heads to pray!

We may be tempted to laugh, or possibly be moved to tears, at such ignorance of the truths of God's word, but this evangelist had no Bible to guide him. He honestly believed that what he had experienced was direction from God to follow the course of action he did.

The results of ignorance of God's word can be far more dramatic than that. One report told of a farmer who, at his baptism, believed that he should see the Holy Spirit in visible form as a dove, just as Jesus had done. On failing to receive such a revelation, he went again and again under the water — until eventually he drowned.

Such examples of zeal without understanding are the exception rather than the rule, but they are not unrepresentative of a church that it still trying to recover from the aftermath of the Cultural Revolution.

Another problem arising from time to time because of the lack of sound teaching is that people seek after all kinds of signs, and want to hear a voice telling them what to do. They often end up hearing the voice of Satan. One man thought he heard the Lord instruct him to offer up his son, in the same way that Abraham was told to offer Isaac. If he did this, then he would see his son raised from the dead. He did as he thought he had been instructed, but when his son failed to rise from the dead, the father shot and killed himself. This incident brought much disgrace to the gospel.

All kinds of extremes have come to the fore. Some groups do not accept the authority of the Old Testament. Other groups place an unhealthy emphasis on dreams, visions and miracles, often using them as their main source of guidance, rather than the Scriptures, which for many are unobtainable.

From Shandong came a report of a church that actually openly opposed Christianity. It claimed there was no salvation to be found in Christianity, and as a result, 300 people have been totally deluded. Other Christians who do not understand the truth have turned to this church.

Into the same province came two Christians from another province, teaching that Christ would return on a certain date. This heresy has split the local house churches which had worked together in harmony since the Cultural Revolution.

In Anhui province two pastors preached that, in order to be saved, one must see a great light as the apostle Paul did while he was travelling on the road to Damascus. Not only that, further requirements were that one must put on sackcloth, sit down in ashes and confess one's sins. After the departure of these two pastors, fierce arguments arose in the church. Some people held firmly to the teaching of Scripture, saying, "We are saved by the grace of God, and by faith." Some agreed with them, others did not. Many lost their faith in God. A once vibrant church now faced the prospect of having meetings that nobody wanted to lead, and in which no-one wanted to learn the word of God. The meetings were no longer taken seriously, the church had no leaders, and the people were like sheep without a shepherd.

These examples are but a sample of the type of heresies and false doctrines that are springing up in the church. They are clearly a work of the enemy to try and hinder the flow of what God is doing. What is the answer? We must help, and we must help now. The Western church has the resources to be able to supply Chinese Christians with some of the Bibles and teaching materials that they so urgently need and to help through radio and other ministries.

It is obvious, from the letters that pour into the Hong Kong ministries' offices, that the Chinese are only too aware of the desperate situation in which they find themselves. Many of those attempting to lead churches are not highly educated people, and because of this are often more aware of their need to understand the word of God clearly. I shall close this section with a few of those letters, which I trust will help to give some idea of the heartcry of our fellow believers behind the Bamboo Curtain. Please let their heartcry touch your heart.

"The Bible said 'If there are several people with true hearts together, God will be with them.' So I went to find another Christian of our village and together we set up a church. Because God was with us, the church expanded every day. The number of people believing in God increased in one year from several persons to two hundred and more.

At that time, the authorities persecuted to stop us trusting in the Lord. They fined us two hundred dollars, and detained us without investigation. Brothers and sisters prayed with one heart to ask God to help us. Our God the Father listened to our prayers, and fulfilled our hope, triumphed over all sorts of hardships, and showed that we were His chosen people. So we came again to His face. Now there are four to five hundred brothers and sisters in our church. People are many, but the Bibles are very few, only several New Testaments and two Old Testaments. Our greatest problem is that we are all new believers, without older believers. So we don't understand the wonders of the Bible."

"I am a young Christian who joined the church only two months ago. I have only a shallow knowledge of the glorious almighty God. I believe Jesus Christ is my Saviour. The pastor asked me to be pastor of his small church. But my knowledge of God is inadequate, and I am in lack of resources and materials."

3. The third reason for helping China is the huge harvest field of unreached men and women that still exists in China today.

There are many areas of China that are still relatively untouched by the Gospel. One of the reasons that I hesitate to give the accounts of revival that I have shared above is that, instead of inspiring us to cry more and reach out for the 950,000,000 men and women and children in China without Christ, we may simply be lulled into feeling there is nothing left to do. We can rejoice at the fruit that we are hearing about in China, but we should not forget that even 50 million Christians is only five percent of the population.

Revival has not yet touched all of China's provinces, and has not yet affected both the cities and the countryside in the same way. In many areas of city and countryside alike there are few believers. Oh that we would rise up and fan the flames of revival for them, by investing now in China. Could we not see the first 50 million as a down payment, a tithe only of what God wants to do in China. One billion people, were they aware of their desperate plight, would surely plead with us to do so.

There is a great spiritual vacuum and hunger for

spiritual reality throughout China. But who or what will fill it? Will Marxism? Hardly — it is a failed and discredited god. Now the Open Door policy has also allowed in other contestants in the battle for the souls of the Chinese, other undesirable gods of Western culture, such as materialism. The greatest dangers facing the house churches in China may not be persecution, opposition or control by the State, but the materialism that is slowly infiltrating the country from the West. How we need to flood in various kinds of evangelistic, apologetic and teaching materials with which to put firm foundations of truth into people's lives.

Is the church in China to be defeated by materialism, because we did not give them the truth while the flame was burning bright?

The traditional religions of Buddhism and Taosim are also capitalising on the situation and making strong efforts to find a place in the hearts of the Chinese. They want to fill the spiritual vacuum. Will the church be able to rise to the challenge? The Chinese Christians are certainly willing, but lack so many of the basic materials needed to follow up their evangelistic successes.

70,000 Salar people in Gansu and Qinghai are of Mongolian origin, but Muslims by religion. As far as is known, they are totally untouched by the gospel to date.

The Mongols have their own state, the Mongolian People's Republic, which is a satellite of the Soviet Union. More Mongols live in China, however, than in their own People's Republic, and most of these live in Inner Mongolia. For centuries they have resisted the gospel. Any attempts at evangelisation have proved largely futile and have left little impression. Today they are one of the major unreached people groups in the world. Yet there are those who urgently want to set up radio work for them, and translate Scriptures for them, but need funding for such projects.

Although the gospel has penetrated many of the tribal people in some regions, there are 1.4 million Yi people in the Daliangshan region of southern Sichuan, mainly living in the remote mountain areas, who still remain totally unreached by the gospel.

There are 6 million Uighur people in Xinjiang province who remain staunchly Muslim and unevangelised. What about those who have never heard? There are nine Muslim peoples in the Xinjiang area of China. Only amongst the largest, the Uighurs, have there ever been churches, and now there are none — they were persecuted out of existence by the Muslims. There are then 6,300,000 Uighurs there without Christ and without hope — as well as about 1.5 million amongst the other Muslim groups in that one province alone. That does not sound like revival to me. But perhaps it could be — if we invest in the flame now.

3-4 million Tibetans live in Qinghai province, but there is little evidence that there are any Christians among them. Tibetan Buddhism has virtually become a world-wide religion, with centres in many countries, yet Tibet itself remains very resistant to the gospel of Christ.

The population of the remote northern province of Ningxia is about 3.9 million. Of these, 1.2 million are Muslim. The capital of the province is Yinchuan, with a population of about 670,000, and according to reports received, only 300 people confess Christ in this city. According to TSPM sources, there are only 1,000 Christians in the whole of Ningxia.

From these few facts and figures, it can be clearly seen that in spite of the explosive growth being experienced, the majority of the 67 million minority peoples and of the 950 million Han Chinese remain totally unevangelised.

These figures are quite staggering if one allows the full import to sink in. One fifth of the world's population is confined within the borders of this one country. There is no larger harvest to be reaped in any other nation on earth. In spite of all the restrictions, the Chinese Christians are doing their utmost, often at great personal cost, to spread the good news of new life in Jesus. But they cannot do it completely alone. They need help from their fellow believers outside of China.

Foreigners cannot go as missionaries to China, but we can support the church there and help her to fulfil the Great Commission. The challenge before us is of a church moving in great power, while at the same time various parts of the body of Christ are being torn apart by heresy and false teaching; of a harvest that is truly ready to be reaped, while the labourers and the tools are insufficient. This is the challenge that lies at the feet of our churches — churches which overflow with resources in terms of people and material. Will we respond? Will we share our bread with the hungry?

The need to learn to invest aright; the need to avoid heresy; the need to sow and reap in this, the greatest harvest in the world today. What then will you say to all these things, fellow servant of the Lord of the harvest field? Are my reasons sufficient, or do you still ask: Why should we respond specifically to China?

Then let my more persuasive friend John Angell James repeat himself once more from the grave:

"The conversion of China is, one way or other, the business of every Christian upon earth — and every Christian upon earth can do something for it and ought to do what he can. The man who says 'What have I to do with this matter?' is either ignorant, indolent or covetous and is altogether heartless towards the cause of Christ. He that says 'What concern have I in China's conversion?' just asks the question 'What fellowship have I with Christ?' We are all too apt to think of what the church can do and ought to do and not what we individually can do and ought to do, and either through modesty, timidity or avarice, lose ourselves and our individual obligations in the crowd. Do you then ask whose business the conversion of China is, I answer, 'yours whosoever you are who may read this page. Yours,' I say, 'as truly as that of any other man on the face of the earth. Here it is, I offer it to you, and in the Name of Christ bid you take it. Take it

178

into your hand, your heart, your purse, your closet — you dare not refuse it'!"

CHAPTER 13

LESSONS TO BE LEARNED
CHINA'S OTHER HEARTCRY

Have Chinese Christians something to say to us? It would be easy to assume — granted the major and pressing needs that I have outlined — that it is all one way traffic. Are we outside of China — sometimes with our long Christian histories and social or cultural assimilations of Christian values — the givers and the Chinese the takers? Are we the missionaries and they the mission fields? Or are there lessons that we can learn from the church in China?

Having seen how we can serve the church in China, and indeed China itself, are there characteristics of Chinese Christians that we would profit from if they were incorporated into our own church and individual lives?

I believe that there are. We must listen and learn in humility, for not only will that enhance our own spiritual effectiveness, but it will prepare us much more thoroughly to serve the church in China.

God has painted a picture of church life on the Chinese canvass that we **must** study. In His wisdom, He has chosen the largest canvass in the world on which to paint

— the most populous nation on the face of the earth. He has also, because of the bamboo curtain, made it one that we have to search for. It is not easy to find and analyse. It is not on the normal Christian tourist route. Indeed, as I have pointed out, it is hard to find at all. Many Christian leaders go to China and conclude that there is no house church movement, though it is flourishing sometimes in the very cities where they stay and in the vast countryside over which they fly. Few Western Christians have the opportunity to visit house churches and sit at the feet of the leaders. But then the pearl of great price was like that — hard to find and costly to buy.

I have already observed that the balance of evangelical Christianity has shifted away from the West. From 1 percent (according to Patrick Johnstone of WEC) in 1800, the 'other' non-Western nations now comprise 60 percent or probably more of those who love the Lord Jesus. But that is not the most vital point. The key issue is that they have left us behind, and continue to stretch away from us in this late stage of the race before the Lord Jesus returns, because they have embraced a different and more Biblical Christianity.

It is not enough for us to sit under some conveniently applied doctrine of the sovereignty of God. That will not do. We need to look at these canvasses in China and Korea and Africa and South America. We need to come under the yoke of change.

For some of us the issue is a simple one. Go back to the Scriptures; obtain a cross-reference from lands like China; and then change and be changed.

I think that it was Malcolm Muggeridge who observed that you could boil a frog to death without the frog trying to escape. You simply place it in cold water and then — very, very gradually — increase the heat under the water until it reaches the temperature that will kill the frog. I do not know if that is true, but I do know that the picture is a good one for many of the churches in the lands where you and I live. If we do not jump clear from our materialism and self-centredness (where the heart of the matter is not the church invading the world but the world invading the church), we will run the risk of boiling to death. Praise God that we yet walk under the grace of the Lord Jesus Christ and hope for His mercy.

If we do not choose to obey the Lord Jesus, the Lord of the church, may help us to do so — with some of the same methods that He has used in China.

This too is the heartcry of China.

I must make two further points before I begin to discuss eight of the lessons we must learn from China's church.

Firstly, the church in China is like any other church. It has good and bad, triumph and dismal failure, honour and dishonour. I am seeking to draw out lessons that are sufficiently true to make them noteworthy. I am not trying to say that every, or even most, of China's Christians always live this way. I do not wish to present a false triumphalism.

Secondly, I am much indebted to many who have gone before me for much of the material in this chapter — and indeed in the whole book. David Adeney of OMF; David Wang of Asian Outreach ("8 Lessons We can Learn From The Church In China"); Jonathan Chao; Dennis Balcombe; Ted Hsueh of Christian Communications Ltd; Ken Lo of FEBC; Tony Lambert and a host of precious OMF brethren...Were I to go on, the list would be as long as the chapter. Thank you, brethren.

1. Their willingness to be a suffering church, with an understanding of the place of obedience to the Lordship of Christ.

Out of times of severe testing, awful tribulation and fierce persecution, God has brought forth a Chinese church full of the power of the Holy Spirit. Persecution and suffering have purified them. The majority of the

183

genuine leaders who are respected today are those who have experienced terrible suffering, imprisonment, humiliation and even torture at the hands of the authorities.

In the current social and religious climate of the West, it is very easy for us to consign the Bible's teaching about suffering to a bygone age. But the word of God says that "everyone who wants to live a godly life in Christ Jesus will be persecuted" (2 Tim 3:12). Jesus certainly left us under no illusions. He spoke of the need to take up the cross daily, of being blessed when — not if — men persecute us and say all manner of things against us. The experience of the early church and church history after that emphatically confirm this truth. Yet some of us today seem almost to believe that suffering might be a suggestion of God's disapproval — that it ought not to happen if we are 'spiritual'! How we need to learn from our Chinese brethren here.

The Christians there have, in the words of Scripture, been armed with a mind to suffer. They know what price there is to pay for following Christ. They are aware that the moment they confess Christ they are putting themselves on a potential collision course with the Marxist authorities. Many still remember the humiliation, rejection, degradation, detention, mental and physical torture and separation from family and loved ones experienced during the Cultural Revolution. After such experiences, nothing comes as a surprise. Persecution and suffering are accepted as the norm for anyone who is serious about their commitment to the cause of Christ.

A former leader of a church in China, who now works in Hong Kong for one of the China ministries, was imprisoned for eighteen years himself. He has a younger brother who still travels the countryside of China as an itinerant evangelist. When asked where his younger brother operated, he pointed to dozens of different locations, spread over a very wide area. When asked why his brother seemed to be constantly on the move, covering such large distances, he said that it was "to keep ahead of the police." Arrest by the police would mean certain detention, but he continues with the work that God has given to him, prepared to accept the consequenees of his actions.

Another itinerant evangelist was interviewed by someone from a Christian organisation in the West. She had spent six years in prison, from 1978 until 1984, because of her continual witnessing and preaching the gospel.

In the prison she continued to witness, although there was a particularly vicious punishment to be endured for anyone who was caught witnessing to others. On one occasion she was caught witnessing. She was taken outside of the prison on a bitterly cold winter's day, to the edge of a strip of land about two kilometres long. Her hands were handcuffed behind her back and her shoes removed. She was then commanded to walk across this strip of land that was covered with razor sharp rocks, something like a beach full of very sharp broken shells.

Before she had gone barely twenty yards, her feet were pouring with blood. Inside of herself, however, she found faith to continue and bear the punishment. The pain became intense and her feet were being cut to shreds. She was leaving pieces of flesh behind with each step. She began to fear that her feet would have to be amputated once the punishment had been completed.

In her moment of acute agony, she began to grumble against God. Why had he allowed her to suffer in this way? Did he not care about the awful pain she was enduring? Then she began to focus her mind on Jesus. With considerable effort she was able to do this at first, but before too long the picture of Jesus on the cross began to fill her mind and imagination. Compared with the unbelievable suffering of Christ, she saw her own pain as insignificant. He had died from His wounds, she would not. There was a crowd of hostile people around

Him, mocking and jeering at Him. She was left almost alone to suffer. He had huge, rough nails hammered through His feet. Hers were 'only' lacerated.

As she dwelt upon the crucifixion scene, somehow the pain in her own feet began to subside. Miraculously she could hardly feel the razor-like rocks. She was able to walk normally over them and cover the distance quickly.

Such incidents are gruesome and repugnant to most people, but they are not so rare in a country that is committed to seeing Christianity eventually eradicated from national life. Whether the persecution takes the form of physical or mental torture, detention, confiscation of belongings (including Bibles and Christian literature) or the banning of meetings, the suffering is real.

Some Chinese Christians view such suffering and opposition in a positive light. They have a different perception and understanding about the Lordship of Jesus Christ. They believe that as Lord, Jesus has the right to do with their lives as he wishes. They must be willing to be used in any way that He desires. If that includes suffering, then they must accept it in faith. It is not unusual to hear pastors and leaders, who have suffered imprisonment for the gospel's sake, refer to their time in the labour camps as their Bible School in the wilderness.

Even young children display an amazing understanding of the issues involved. The children of one family, when asked, "Aren't you sad that your father has been in prison for such a long time?", replied: "How else would those in prison have been able to hear the Gospel of Jesus?" It is a fact of recent decades that many in China's prisons and detention camps have found Christ through the willingness of believers to accept unjust imprisonment with grace, and see in it the purposes of God — that He had put them there to reach the other-wise unreachable. How else could Paul have reached the Philippian jailer in Acts 16?

It was summed up for me by the testimony told to me in Southern China by an elderly preacher. He had been admitted to hospital, but had released himself so that he could go to preach in a church some distance from where he lived. He was still quite unwell, but knew how much the congregation in that particular town eagerly awaited his visit.

After an uncomfortable journey in an old bus, he found many people waiting, eager for God's word. After the teaching, he would normally stay behind to minister, but on this occasion, tired and ill, he left at once. He thankfully boarded a waiting bus and was relieved to find an empty seat. He sat down, grateful that he did not have to stand on the two hour journey to his home town.

As the bus was about to leave, a lady climbed on board and begged him to return and minister to a sick brother. His pleas regarding his own health were of no avail and he reluctantly returned.

Later he caught the next bus, which had no vacant seat! One hour down the road they came across the earlier bus, completely overturned. There was every chance that he might have been killed were he to have travelled on it. As he surveyed the scene, He felt the Spirit of God speak to him: "Don't always be considering the demands of your own flesh, but put the work of the Lord first!"

We may find that very hard. I have sometimes said that, were the Holy Spirit to confront us in that way, we might ask Him to leave! Yet this attitude is found over and over again in the lives of many Chinese Christians. There is a spirit of self-denial running through much that is done in the church in China.

I must add a last word. They are not super-saints, some breed of men and women apart. I have seen them glance behind for the dark shadow, knowing what another arrest can bring. I believe, however, that, generally speaking, they have accepted two keys, two great spiritual secrets.

187

Firstly, that for Christians to suffer in some way or another is normal (cf 2 Tim 3:12 above).

Secondly, that the grace of God is sufficient for them. He will give them all the grace they need (cf Phil 4:10-13). So they are not the key to victory. He, the Lord Jesus, is. We can walk in that way to, if we obey those two simple steps — releasing ourselves from our self-centredness and walking in His sufficiency.

I talked with a brother in central China who had walked through the bad times. He had been made to stand up to his neck in freezing mid-winter in a lake. They wanted to kill him, but he meditated on the Psalms and the Lord kept him. This dear brother, as we shared, simply observed: "Sometimes it is easier, sometimes it is harder; but we learn to know the times and the seasons, and to walk accordingly". May God help us so to do.

2. Their vital commitment to fervent prayer.

All that Chinese Christians do flows from a foundation of prayer. They have learnt how to pray out of sheer necessity. When the authorities removed the church leaders and imprisoned them, the only thing left for those in prison, and the congregations they had left, was to pray fervently. The lessons they learnt through prayer have held them in good stead, and a church has been raised on committed, intercessory prayer. It is a vital part of their life — many would say their lifeblood — out of which all their decisions, plans and activities are born.

Dennis Balcombe was invited, on one of his numerous trips into mainland China, to attend a baptismal service. This was highly unusual, as normally house church leaders do not invite foreigners to any services, let alone an outdoor meeting of this nature.

When he arrived in the town, he realised that he still had three hours before the baptismal service was due to begin in the local river. Consequently he decided to spend some time alone on the riverbank, enjoying the quiet of the surroundings. As he drew near to the river, he noticed a number of cycles standing on the bank. The closer he got, the more cycles became visible, until it was apparent that there were rows and rows of them stacked together. Then he saw the owners of the machines. Hundreds of young people were gathered by the river, not out for a picnic, or barbecue, but to pray.

The scene was unforgettable. This great crowd of youngsters were kneeling, praying fervently, seeking God with all earnestness for their nation, asking for the salvation of many people.

Dennis arrived just after 4pm. The baptismal service was due to begin at 7pm. The young people continued praying aloud as one voice until the time of the service. At 7pm the leader stood and officially began the meeting. He suggested that they should begin with prayer, and once again hundreds of voices were lifted to heaven in intercessory prayer. The initial time of prayer continued unabated until 11.30pm, at which time the baptisms began. Several hundred people were baptised.

Is it any wonder that such a mighty revival is sweeping through the land, with this kind of commitment to prayer being the rule rather than the exception?

A well known Chinese pastor was given permission to attend a conference where a number of leaders from the West were in attendance. On his way home he was asked what he thought about the conference. He considered the question for some time, and then, without any sense of wishing to criticise or be judgmental, simply said, "My brothers in the West know how to plan, and that is good; but we know how to pray."

During the dark periods, they meet in small groups of two or three, or, if possible, in larger groups. The main emphasis of their time together is prayer. They cling to the throne of heaven, and storm the gates of hell with their intercession. Because prayer has become the main focus of their times together when persecution is fierce, it remains so in other seasons too. Praying for three or four hours is not unusual. They have learned to persist in prayer, over long periods of time, until they see their requests answered.

Many of China's Christians are virtually forced into an attitude of prayer over many aspects of their lives. The majority are extremely poor and are therefore totally dependent upon their heavenly Father to meet their daily needs. They pray about everything and anything that affects their lives including, in rural areas, animals that are sick or lost.

Prayer is as natural as breathing to them. They do not miss any opportunity to lift their hearts to God, and it could be honestly said of them that they have learnt the art of praying without ceasing.

Jonathan Chao of the Chinese Church Research Centre, a courageous and godly brother whom I rejoice to call a friend, has spoken of a house church meeting he attended in 1987. It was a time of much confusion arising from a new wave of persecution — many of the younger evangelists were low in spirit. The believers had gathered for a special meeting in a cave 25 feet below ground level. After three messages lasting for well over three hours, they began to pray — "that is their pattern", said Jonathan. "After hearing the message, they prayed, with tears running down from their eyes, and the stream of tears intermingled with their 'noserun', dripping down like transparent noodles, which they ignored. For their hearts were so turned to the face of Christ that they became totally oblivious of their own unkempt state. One sister prayed for over 45 minutes standing, pleading with the Lord to release her fellow-evangelist and her fiance from prison. He had fasted for many days and refused to divulge any information on the churches' evangelistic activity."

You and I must learn together the primacy of the place of prayer. When the story is told, I believe that God's evaluation of what constitutes a successful church will be very different from ours. Samuel Chadwick was right when he said that "prayer is the acid test of devotion".

190

That means the Chinese church is proving their devotion in prayer. Are we?

3. Their commitment to the Bible.
The word of God is held in great esteem and highly cherished among house church Christians. Bibles are still very scarce in some areas and there is a great hunger amongst the people of God for the Scriptures. It is not merely for the pleasure of being able to read the Bible that these Christians long to own a copy. They are desperate to understand God's heart on many issues. They want to be doers of the word, not merely hearers. There are many issues about which there is contention, and they long to understand God's word in order that clarity might be brought to the situation and that truth might reign.

Bibles are like gold dust, virtually unobtainable for many Christians. That is why portions of Scripture are still copied out by hand, many times over, and distributed to as many people as possible. These portions will sometimes be memorised thoroughly. You discover just how much has been remembered when they pray — for the word of God is liberally mixed into the prayers!

Chinese Christians love God's word. They will travel hundreds of miles to obtain a copy of the Bible. They will go for long distances by foot or bicycle just to hear an itinerant evangelist preach. Once they are in a meeting, they drink in the word of God. They are more than happy to sit and listen for hour upon hour. Often they will not let preachers stop, but encourage them to give all that they have, until the preachers are exhausted.

David Wang recounts a visit he made to the city of Xian to meet a relatively new convert who had begged him to let her do something for God in the way of distributing Bibles and tapes. He was due to meet her at 9pm, but she did not arrive until 1am. She was delayed because she had been delivering some Bibles in a village not far from their meeting place. The local authorities

191

had discovered what she was doing, however, and had beat her up, robbed her and left her on a deserted road. Still she kept her appointment with David.

Apart from the beating she did not look at all well. When David asked what was wrong with her, she showed him her legs that were covered with stings and mosquito bites. This was part of her price for travelling in remote parts of the countryside delivering God's word. She had to sleep in huts or open fields, attacked by many insects. David urged her to go to a doctor with him, but she refused. She explained that she had to leave the next morning for Inner Mongolia with the Bibles that David had brought to her.

Not long after that she disappeared and nothing was heard from her for some time. Later David received a small piece of paper smuggled through by some friends of hers. On it was written the news that she had been arrested and charged with 'distributing superstitious materials'. A few weeks later news filtered through that this twenty-four year old young woman, who had given all her energy to delivering the word of God, so desperately needed by Christians, had been executed. She had been able to answer the question in the affirmative. The word of God was worth dying for.

How much value do we place on the word of God? How central is it to our lives? Do we long for the purifying word to do its work in our lives? When we are faced with opposition, ridicule, contempt, adversity and persecution, do we believe that this revelation from the living God is really worth making the ultimate sacrifice for?

4. Their sensitivity To The Holy Spirit.

Christians in China have lived through many years of suffering, times when they walked a very lonely and dangerous path. In order to survive the tremendous difficulties they had to develop a very fine tuned ear to the voice of God. Sometimes, it was virtually impossible to let people know when a meeting would take place. It was up to each individual, therefore, to listen to the Holy Spirit for themselves and discern when and where the meeting would take place.

This sensitivity to God's Spirit is seen in every area of their lives. Jonathan Chao tells of a Christian woman in charge of security at a coal mine. The woman suddenly felt the Holy Spirit urging her to pull the alarm lever, even though there was no apparent reason to do so. Although everything seemed quiet and normal, she obeyed the prompting within her.

The whole mine was evacuated as a result of the alarm sounding, but when all the men had assembled on the surface, it seemed as if a huge mistake had been made. Just moments later the ground beneath their feet shook and a large section of the mine collapsed.

Because of this sister's sensitivity and willingness to obey God, everyone's lives had been saved. Additionally, however, 400 of the miners surrendered their lives to Christ after recognising that God had miraculously saved them from death.

Such sensitivity is not only evident in the lives of adults, but in children too. Their openness to the voice of the Holy Spirit, their willingness to respond to Him, is at times quite amazing. Some children have learnt to discern the genuineness of a visitor to their homes — even though that visitor might claim to be a believer, and make all the right "spiritual noises". They know how to exercise the gift of discernment of spirits (1 Cor 12:10). They hear the Holy Spirit telling them who is to be trusted and who is not. In that way, by listening to the still, small voice of the Holy Spirit, they may protect their parents — who may be leaders in the house church movement.

I feel this too is a key challenge to us in the evangelical church in the West. So much is head communicated and received, and not Holy Spirit communicated and received. Early in the decade of the 80's, I was at a

193

meeting where Western evangelicals sat with certain Chinese church 'leaders'. In fact, those of us who knew the situation knew well that some of the Chinese were not committed Christians at all, but were party men. Yet the fact is that they knew how to use 'spiritual language' in such a way as to deceive some of the Western leaders. That is because the communication of the kind of language we are used to — certain Biblical catch phrases or whatever — convinces us that, if the code words are being given, the values must be identical. May God help us to learn what our Chinese brothers and sisters have had to learn. They know that infiltration of the church involves the assimilation of language and attitudes, without a change of heart and spirit. Thus it is the Holy Spirit who alone can reveal the real state of the spirit and heart of a man, if and when He chooses.

Surely from cover to cover that is a basic Biblical truth. The book of Acts alone is full of it — Peter with Ananias and Sapphira in Acts 5, and with Simon the sorcerer in Acts 8, to mention but two examples.

May our own book of Acts retrieve that spiritual ability soon, as we learn from the Scriptures and the Chinese book of Acts! The stakes are no less vital for us than for them.

5. Their lack of ecclesiastical structures — they are de-institutionalised.

They are free from the institutional and traditional trappings that were sometimes brought to China by us from the West. They have developed their own forms and style of ministry, suitable to the Chinese situation. They are often free to meet where they want or are able, because they are not tied to buildings. In fact, they meet anywhere that is convenient.

They have come to realise the truth of the church being a body of people, not a building, in whom the Spirit of God dwells. In this they have encouraged the priesthood of all believers. Although there are definite leaders, they do not often dominate, either by their gift or personality. The ministry comes from people from all walks of life, people who have been recognised as being faithful and having the necessary gifts for the encouragement and upbuilding of the saints.

The links that churches in China had with various Western denominations before the Communist takeover have been almost entirely severed. Building on the foundation of many godly missionaries, they have drawn strength in God to triumph over this separation. It has produced strength, character and life of enviable quality. Some of the doctrinal or denominational differences of the Western churches now no longer affect a church whose concern is to see unity maintained, believers grow into maturity, and the gospel spread far and wide.

Churches which lost their buildings and their corporate life became centred around and rooted in the family, as meetings had to be held in homes, where often the head of the family would take responsibility for the people gathering under his roof. This lack of structure has proved of enormous benefit to the church in China. It has probably been one of the main reasons for its survival. The flexibility, the purity and the life displayed is a challenge to those of us outside of China who have become ensnared by division, buildings, and other non-essentials that we have come to regard as normal or even vital to the ongoing work of the church.

David Adeney, another godly and precious brother with a Western exterior and a Chinese interior, has often observed that the Chinese have had no eleven o'clock meetings, or committees, or choirs, or fraternals, or anything else! They simply had a first love for the Lord Jesus and a love for one another in Christ — and a love for the lost. Those three 'loves' — those three key relationships — were the ends. The rest — the structures and the ways of doing it — were the means. That is one of the reasons why they see revival and we do not. We have fallen into the trap of submerging the ends and of almost worshipping the means!

6. Their belief in the ministry of the Holy Spirit in the realm of the miraculous and of His gifts — and also of His fruit.

Healings, miracles, signs and wonders are the norm for the Christians of China. They believe Jesus when He said that His followers would do even greater things than He had done. They are not taken completely by surprise when people are raised from the dead, delivered from evil spirits or healed of all kinds of diseases. They do not need books and teaching material telling them how to get into this kind of ministry, for they practise it as part of their everyday life in Christ.

It is often the miracles that are the means of influencing non-Christians to consider seriously the claims of the gospel. A surgeon performed an operation on an elderly lady who had a severe case of cancer of the colon. He was a Christian and was a distant relative of the lady. He showed the case history and X-rays to the other surgeons in the hospital before performing the operation, but also prayed much for his relative. When he actually came to carry out the operation, he was somewhat surprised to find every trace of the cancer gone.

The other doctors were shown this, and the X-rays were again studied to ensure that there had been no mistake. There was little doubt that a miracle had taken place, and as a result many of his colleagues are now open to listening to the Christian doctor about his faith. The whole family of the woman concerned also came to acknowledge the lordship of Jesus because of her healing.

Church life in China can seem like stepping back into the pages of the New Testament. A little boy who had been dead for over ten hours was brought back to life by the persistent prayers of a mother who refused to accept that it was the right time for him to die. The boy's father came to faith in Christ because of this (whereas he had previously told the mother to take the dead boy and depart from him, such was his grief at losing his precious and only son). Together they travelled around the district telling what a marvellous thing the Lord had done for them. They were joined by an evangelistic team who helped them to present the gospel. Within one month over 4,000 people became Christians.

Such experiences are relatively commonplace and a prominent feature of the current move of the Holy Spirit in China. For Chinese Christians it would be considered strange if signs and wonders did not accompany the preaching of the gospel. Compare this to much of what happens in the West, and it is understandable that we should feel our poverty and lack in this area. For all our conferences on signs and wonders, our seminars on healing and deliverance, and the mountain of literature that is produced on these subjects, we have yet to experience the supernatural power of the Holy Spirit in quite the same way as our Chinese brethren.

Why is this? Perhaps it has something to do with the uncomplicated, childlike faith of the Chinese believers. They trust God and His word implicitly. They do not doubt for one moment that He wants to manifest His power in and through their lives. They simply go out and trust and obey! They have nothing else to trust in. Blessed indeed are the poor! Their trust in God is enough to see miracles abound and lives challenged and brought face to face with the living God as a result.

But there is a sting in the tail here. It is not just the gifts of the Spirit — the miraculous — that has brought this change. The cumbersome title to this section is intended to stress to you that they major on the fruit of the Spirit (Gal 5:22-23) as well as the gifts of the Spirit (1 Cor 12:7-11 etc). I shall address the question of that fruit briefly in a section below. But it is vital to stress that their growth in and through evangelism has been through a balance in these two elements of the supernatural — charisma and character if you will — and not just through the one.

7. Their commitment to evangelism at all costs.

China is undoubtedly witnessing a revival of unprecedented proportions. The Holy Spirit is sweeping across the land, affecting whole villages, communities and towns. People are coming out of darkness into the glorious light of God's kingdom in numbers that are almost difficult to imagine. The fire of God's love is being kindled in hearts that were disillusioned, and bound up by fear and superstition. Where once there was outright opposition to the gospel, now there is glad surrender to the Lord Jesus Christ, even in the hearts of Party workers and officials.

Coupled with this amazing move of God's Spirit, however, is the willingness of the Chinese church to accept its part in helping to spread the flame. In spite of all the opposition and restrictions placed upon them, Christians have almost always found ways of witnessing When the political situation eases, they simply take full advantage and engage in aggressive evangelism.

Itinerant evangelists risk everything to reach those who have never heard the good news of Jesus. They travel from town to town, and village to village, often keeping just one step ahead of the authorities. In many instances they see an incredible response to their preaching. They begin a new church, give the new converts a few days of instruction in the word of God, then move on to the next place. The courage of these itinerant evangelists is beyond dispute. Banned by the authorities and the TSPM, these dedicated men and women risk everything for the sake of taking the gospel to areas where Christ is not acknowledged. Often with little financial support, away from family and friends, they travel for weeks and months, sharing the good news. If caught, they are dealt with in no uncertain terms by the authorities, and they are, therefore, constantly having to stay alert to danger of this kind.

People who are recognised as having a calling as an evangelist are encouraged into their ministry, and will often try to find jobs that will bring them into contact with people as much as possible. In this way they will have above average opportunity to bring the message of God's love to unbelievers. All church members seek to be witnesses, however. Even if they are unable to do so openly, they quietly share their faith with relatives and friends, and a great harvest is being reaped by these methods.

Even during the darkest days of the Cultural Revolution, when fear dominated the atmosphere, Christians often showed by their lifestyle, their love, care and concern for others, that Jesus was a living reality. Their example in showing compassion, even towards those who persecuted them and their families, was the means of leading others to Christ, including fanatical Red Guards.

In a city in Southern China I dropped into the TSPM church one evening. There was an evangelistic meeting going on. The speaker was a woman from one of the house churches in the area which had joined together with the TSPM. They felt at ease in an environment when they could do the Lord's work with relative freedom. She preached the Gospel with a directness and a clarity that I have seldom heard in the West — making it clear that there was no other way to be saved and find life than that of the Lord Jesus. Sharing with her privately after the meeting, I saw too that she had another way of winning souls, as so many have in China. She said that many came to her in the factory where she worked with their problems. They knew that something was different, and were drawn by the love and the light of the Lord Jesus which they saw, not just in the church, but also in the workplace. The fruit of the Spirit in her life attracted others to Christ.

Today the commitment to the great commission is as strong as ever. Chinese Christians are serious about the commands of their Lord, and as a result are seeing a plentiful harvest. Can we in the free nations of the world do less than our Chinese brethren, for whom spreading the gospel is such a high risk business?

8. Their commitment to one another as brethren in Christ.

The believers in China learnt a long while ago that Christianity meant far more than attending meetings regularly. If that was all their faith had consisted of, then it would have indeed died during the dark periods of Chinese history.

Their faith is outworked in many ways, but one of the most significant is in deep fellowship and commitment to their fellow believers. There is an overwhelming sense of care for each other, and a real desire to support those who are struggling for one reason or another, often in very practical but necessary ways.

The support for families who have seen loved ones imprisoned for their beliefs is genuine and exemplary. Even though the vast majority of Christians are poor, even by Chinese standards, they share what they have with others who are in even greater need.

It is not uncommon to hear stories of those imprisoned suffering severe shortages of the very basic necessities of life, yet being willing to give what meagre amounts they had to other prisoners who were weak or ill through lack of food and nourishment.

Such acts of love and care do not go unnoticed. The way that Christians show their commitment to one another is a powerful witness to unbelievers in China, and has resulted in even hardened atheists turning to the living God.

★★★★★★★★★★★★★★★★★★★★★★

None of these attributes of the church in China are cultural. They are scriptural, but not cultural. They are

200

all to be found within the pages of the Bible, and as such, are applicable to all believers everywhere for all time. Much of what we have seen in the lives of these Chinese Christians has been born as a result of intense persecution and suffering. They have been forced into more flexible structures, intense prayer and a hunger for the word of God.

What will have to happen to the church outside of China before we begin to exhibit the kind of lifestyle so evident in China? Or will we, of our own volition and trusting in the grace of God, take active steps towards a spirituality that is consistent with the pages of the New Testament and the heart of God?

Will we learn from them — learn in the way that the Bible means, which of necessity involves observable change? Or will we 'absorb', as we have done so often in recent years, generating short-term interest in place of long-term change. May God have mercy on us — as He has had on them!

CHAPTER 14

BLACK SUN OVER CHINA

"A black sun has appeared in the sky of my motherland. Black sun, I am going to shoot you down".
Wuerkaixi, student leader of the Tiananmen democracy movement after the massacre.

In June 1989 a horrified world watched and listened to the accounts of the Tiananmen massacre. It was different this time. In the past China has murdered and imprisoned behind the impenetrable bamboo curtain. Stories have emerged after the event — stories of horror at inhuman cruelty and sometimes of indescribable human courage. But not this time. This time we watched it unfold before our eyes. It seemed as if we could almost reach out and touch it ourselves.

Above and beyond the horror one fact stands out. There are men in China who were capable and willing to kill in that way for their own political ends, even though they knew that the whole world was watching. They were then prepared to challenge what we had all seen and claim that it had never happened. Fifteen years of apparent change was rolled back before our eyes. We are left with one simple question: has anything —

bar some superficial economic policies — changed in the top leadership in China? That is the question we need to ask here. Are we locked into some ever-recurring cycle in China, or is there, beneath that hard exterior of endless slaughter and inhumanity, something different taking place?

The beginnings of the 1989 democracy movement were humble ones. It even seems that the authorities could have prevented the whole affair if they had moved early enough. One of the earliest of the rallies, which resulted in 100,000 people demonstrating in Tiananmen Square, began nervously at Beijing University. The students had been warned: "If you go out and demonstrate, we can't say what the consequences will be." They delayed for half an hour. The movement, with a little conviction from the Government, could perhaps have been crushed there and then — before it had really begun. But the leadership, perhaps because it was divided by infighting between hardliners and moderates, failed to move. The rest is history — and infamy.

The actual events leading up to the democracy demonstrations were unusual. Three very significant events fell close together, forming a unique opportunity for the students to express themselves and for the movement to gain and sustain momentum. Without these events it is hard to see that it could have reached the level that it did.

The first event was the death of Hu Yaobang. Hu had been General Secretary at the time of the student riots at the end of 1986. He was a man of some integrity; he was also a moderate politically. It is interesting that he did not at any time in recent days come under criticism from the students for corruption, something that could not be said of even his fellow moderate, Zhao Ziyang. Deng Xiaoping blamed Hu for those 1986 riots and stripped him of his position. When Hu died on April 15th, the students began to demand that he be posthumously reinstated, claiming that he had been treated unjustly.

It is likely that the students had already prepared for the second event even before Hu's death. May 4th saw the seventieth anniversary of the May Fourth Movement. George Walden writing in the London "Daily Telegraph" linked it to the political conscience of the nation. 70 years ago, modern China came into existence through a student-led revolt. On May 4th, 1919, detachments of Beijing (then Peking) students, many in traditional robes, marched into the city centre protesting against the Versailles Peace conference, which had confirmed Japan's occupation of Shangtung province, and against the acceptance by China's leaders of Japan's iniquitous 21 demands. The marchers were orderly. The students gave a lead, the country followed. Walden argues that May 4th, 1919, is to be seen as a national rather than ideological movement, and has a deeper appeal than the communist movement of 1949. The key was patriotism. The cause was democratic reform.

The third event was the visit of Soviet President Gorbachev to China on May 15th. Now more than ever the eyes of the world were focussed on the capital. The unprecedented gathering of the world's press for this meeting of the two Communist superpowers focussed our gaze on the city. The students, already in full flow after the first two events, seized the opportunity presented by the Soviet visit so comprehensively that they both upstaged it and caused Gorbachev's programme to have to be altered. I believe that as much as anything that was unforgivable in Deng's eyes. There is evidence for saying that Deng saw the summit as a climax to his long and powerful career. The students shamed him. For that, as well as for all else, they had to be massacred. It was too much. The fire had spread too fast. By May 18th, similar demonstrations had taken place in 24 of the 27 provincial and regional capitals. In Shanghai 100,000 students and supporters forced Gorbachev to cancel part of his itinerary. There was a broadcast of a lecture from a young student on how to run the Communist Party of 47 million members.

At any rate, the result of the three events was that during the second half of May, two million people were on the streets of Beijing in peaceful demonstrations. Witnesses say that the atmosphere was relaxed and happy — the word "carnival" has been used to describe it. The students kept very tight control of events, pouncing quickly on pickpockets if they were caught or, worse still, on any threat to order such as the daubing with paint of Mao's statue in the Square. They had known that, as intellectuals, they could not protest successfully by themselves. The turning point appeared at the time to have been reached when the "workers" came out in support, bringing with them their children. It seemed that a critical point of momentum had been reached that would be hard to stop.

The London Times of May 18th described how Beijing was brought to a standstill. From early morning of Wednesday, May 17th, hundreds of thousands of students, academics, office and factory workers streamed towards Tiananmen Square along roads closed to traffic. By mid-afternoon all the broad avenues leading to the Square were blocked with people, smiling, shouting, waving and talking excitedly. Few policemen were in evidence — some jettisoned their jackets and caps to join the demonstration. The impression was of a city of ten million people given over to the demonstrators. Workers from clothing factories, from publishing houses, from the China International Trade Investment Corporation, musicians and a dance troupe — all were there. Taxi drivers went on strike, buses became vehicles of propaganda, carrying demonstrators. Student stewards and organisers rivalled their government foe in officiousness and bureaucracy. Areas of the Square were cordoned off. Certain cordons required a special pass or registering of time of arrival and departure. Constant confidential meetings to discuss the next move were taking place. Yet on the outer fringe of the Square something like a carnival was taking place. At that high point, The Times asked a significant question: how can a government punish two million marchers?

The Party appeared helpless in the face of it. In retrospect, that was far from the truth. It seems that the security police were active amongst the crowds, waiting for their opportunity to pounce and imprison and kill. But there was no formal crackdown because the top leadership was split. On May 20th Li Peng broadcast a warning that the city was in turmoil. That was untrue. It was in fact the party that was in turmoil, unable to decide what to do as the militants and the moderates fought for control. Months before, the Public Security Bureau had warned the leadership to expect student unrest in May. But it was locked in a bitter power struggle and could not respond.

The hard facts are that if the government had been willing to enter into genuine dialogue, the massacre could have been avoided. Most of the students, including the top leadership in the Square, were not intent on removing the Party. Far from it. It is essential that we who live abroad understand that they wanted to reform the Party, not to overthrow it. I doubt that many even now see the issue as the overthrow of the Party. The students even proclaimed such slogans as: "support the correct policies of the Communist Party; support socialism; long live the Party." Now, after the massacre, the expressed (or repressed) desire of almost all is the removal of the Li Peng, Deng Xiaoping and Yang Shangkun element out of leadership. Indeed, the students took great care not to give offence — until the massacre had begun. The whole situation could have been resolved by genuine discussion about the issues at hand.

The original central demands from the students, forming the basis of the May 13th Tiananmen Square sit-in hunger strike, two days before Gorbachev's arrival, were:

i)   Full recognition of the unofficial student's union formed the previous month.

ii)   Meaningful negotiations, to be televised live, between students and Party leaders.

iii)   Official retraction of the condemnation of student unrest carried by the People's Daily on April 26th.

Behind these key demands lay anger at corruption amongst Party officials and similar matters. One leader spoke to Li Peng, saying: "The biggest problem is corruption among officials. To solve this corruption, they must begin with their own sons. What people hate most is corruption. If you want to have prestige, then the top officials should begin by dealing with their own sons."

The Party chose not to enter into dialogue. The old bloodthirsty Stalinists who have gained control in these days, with Li Peng as the front man, do not understand that kind of language. The Party leadership was forced to this place by a dilemma over its economic policies. As I have said elsewhere, the post-1978 period in China has been the era of the Four Modernisations. Yet for all the economic changes, Deng was determined that there should be no political changes. Sooner or later the two conflicting forces — political and economic — had to collide. They did so in the Square, helped on by raging inflation and the feeling that genuine economic change could never come without political change. Deng had to decide whether power for himself or progress for China mattered most to him. He made his choice and the students picked up the price tag with their lives. The irony there is that those who died were some of the most promising products of the Deng era. It was Deng's reforms that had awakened the desire for a cessation of corruption and a democratic voice in the processes of government.

The crime of those who were awakened was that they were more logical and honest than Deng in pursuit of those matters. The conclusion, even before the massacre, came from a leading Chinese dissident, the astrophysicist Fang Lizhi. He argued that there could be no further political change in China till Deng was dead. That made the movement in May and June premature and doomed. Deng's only official post is that of Chief of the Military Affairs Commission. At the height of the troubles he travelled to Wuhan and summoned the key army commanders. In retrospect, now that the reports of potential army infighting seem to have come to nothing, we can see the Deng held the trump cards in the struggle and was never likely to lose unless he had died or was removed.

In my view the student movement, in the form it took, was doomed to failure, though I do not believe that of the factors which lay behind it. I know that it is easy to be wise after the event. But I must ask you to allow me that luxury!

Firstly, there was no coherent political direction in which they were going. They were more clear about what was wrong (corruption, lack of freedom of the press and so on) than they were about what could replace it in a systematic way. Witnesses have spoken of anarchy, nihilism, elements of humanist and other Marxist traditions. I believe that it is arguable that some in the Square had little idea as to why they were there, except that they longed for change — and enjoyed the breath of clearer air that blew through China in those few short weeks. News Network International carried a report of one person who, when asked what she was doing there, said that the issue was her watch — it did not work. Into the Square came almost an oriental sense of dying for the cause without necessarily knowing for which cause they were dying. Who could take the place in the vacuum? As the London Times observed, were it not for the fact that there was no obvious alternative, it would have been possible to predict the collapse of the leadership. Deng had earned the contempt of the people. Li Peng had strengthened his reputation as an incompetent leader without imagination. Zhao Ziyang was possibly in the strongest position, but had predicted there would be no more large scale demonstrations, and looked a little ridiculous.

Secondly, it never ceases to amaze me that Chinese young people have such short memories. They either have never faced up to the facts of the past, or have not chosen to remember them. The Cultural Revolution and other gross violations and killings do not seem to leave their mark on the consciousness of the young. Videos after the event point to their surprise that the hardliners would have given the order to open fire. But why? They have done it before, and they will do it again, if they are allowed to do so.

I talked after the massacre with one scholar in the West. Shocked by the atrocities, she yet hankered for Mao's days. I expressed surprise, given the fact that Mao was responsible for many more deaths than she had seen in the Square. She looked at me and, without a glimmer of untruth in face and voice, denied that Mao has ever been responsible for such atrocities. In one generation the villain may again become hero, especially when contrasted with today's villains. Perhaps the next generation will come to see and understand the rules — or the lack of them — by which this fearful game is played. This one does not seem to have done.

For the present, China faces another horrific purge, perhaps on the level of the Cultural Revolution or those that took place at Liberation. The usual gruesome litany unfolds before our eyes: hundreds have been arrested; scores executed, usually with the bullet to the back of the head, victims sometimes picked seemingly at random out of the crowd; relative betrays relative; fear reigns supreme. An intellectual, writing to a friend in the West, cried out that the "air" was so heavy that they could hardly breath. The state-controlled media have thrown a total blanket over the nation, claiming that the massacre never took place. There was, so it is said, an armed counter-revolutionary rebellion away from the Square. Only several hundred died, many of them soldiers who were using maximum restraint, and also some innocent bystanders. The students, so the official version runs, left the Square peacefully, banners and flags still in their hands. One scholar told me, holding a Hong Kong newspaper in one hand and a Party controlled one in the other hand, that both versions were equally convincing — unless you really knew the facts.

THE FUTURE.

We cannot say which way China will go in the short or long term. But we can pray and we can act, without waiting to read the signs of the times. I believe that we need now to do more, not less for China.

It is likely that there will be a purge on the church as long as this current group remains in power. There is little doubt that they will clamp down on various sectors of society, including the church. Moreover local leftist cadres will emerge from their tentative postures and attack the churches. It may be a hard time, and we need to pray much for China's Christians.

We need also to give our energies to strengthening the church in China for its primary task of evangelism. The chapters on prayer, radio, literature and other ministries that I have written in this book tell us what is needed. It is simply that we need more of that now!

The Chinese Church Research Centre in Hong Kong reported (CNCR 1379) that one evangelist in Inner Mongolia saw more people became Christians through his efforts during the democracy movement than over the whole of the preceding three years. We do not need to say that the massacre put an end to that; I believe that the opposite is true. We need to see the matter in a quite different light. History has shown that such events in China, such bloodshed and the persecution of all sectors of society, including the church, have led to more being saved in China, and even to revival. I believe that will be the outcome of these horrific events. What hope is there outside of the Prince of Peace?

One praying saint in the West shared that she saw from the Lord that the events resembled the way in which in some parts of the world sugar cane is harvested. The field is first burnt off, so that all that remains is the material to be harvested. Then the cane can be gathered in. China has yet again been burnt with savage fire. But God intends another full harvest of souls where Satan has burnt so savagely. We need to work with all-out effort and all our compassion to see it gathered in.

★★★★★★★★★★★★★★★★★★★★★★

At the start of this chapter I posed a question: has anything — bar some superficial economic policies — changed in the top leadership in China? Are we locked into some ever-recurring cycle of violence in China? Is there, beneath that surface coating of endless slaughter and inhumanity, something different taking place? I need now to address that question.

The horrific actions in the Square may be argued to have had the very opposite effect from that which they intended. As OMF have commented, "the people are politically awake. Morally and politically the Li Peng regime is bankrupt, and although it may cling on to power through brutal force, its days must be numbered. The concept of the Mandate of Heaven is deeply rooted in the Chinese psyche. Throughout history peasants have sensed the impending collapse of a regime because of corruption, inner decay and the loss of the moral right to rule the country. Intellectuals have formed judgments about the legitimacy of a particular dynasty. Ballads and satirical rhymes circulate, and the more superstitious interpret extraordinary natural events as supernatural portents of the collapse of the dynasty.... Recent events in Beijing prove that the Li Peng regime has now also forfeited the Mandate of Heaven in the eyes of the people. A leading Hong Kong political journal had the headline: 'Those whom the gods wish to destroy they first make mad'".

Marlowe Hood of the South China Morning Post has put it this way: "In a month of unprecedented and epochal changes, one stands out above the rest. For the first time since the establishment of the People's Republic of China, the Communist Party is ruling over a hostile population."

The wind of change is not still in China, nor are the hopes of change becalmed. What seems a setback, a reversal, may in fact be the death throes of one era, that of the old men, and the birth of another. The past suggests that is possible. In 1976, there was a remembrance rally in Tiananmen Square for Zhou Enlai, who had just died. The government cracked down. It is said that hundreds or even a few thousand were killed in the same Tiananmen Square at that time. However, within 3 months, the faction of the Communist government that perpetuated the massacre were gone — Chairman Mao had died and the Gang of Four were arrested. Indeed the massive earthquake of that year was seen by some as a portent of the change of Mandate involved in those events.

For the Christian who loves China, however, there must be a different perspective than this alone. There is a vital issue at stake. I have observed that there was a vacuum in the Square — a nihilism sometimes. There was a greater clarity regarding what was opposed than there was about what was to be promoted under the term 'democracy'. Indeed, report after report spoke of an unhealthy vacuum, even amongst the student leaders, as to what 'democracy' might mean. This is the issue that we have to face. We need to pray and labour to fill the vacuum that existed in the Square.

The leading dissident Fang Lizhi, before going into hiding in the US Embassy after the massacre, declared that "Socialism is the scourge of humanity in this

213

century. China has no religion. We need to find a new belief."

A Christian leader, quoted by Open Doors, said: "The significance of the protests lies not so much in what the people were protesting about, but rather in the mere fact that they were protesting. We are not only protesting forty years of Maoism, but 2,500 years of Confucianism. Confucius taught us many wise things, but he also taught us that if a man was old he was also right, and must be respected at all costs. In other words, he taught us not to protest. And now here we are, taking matters into our own hands for the first time in our history. It is revolution!. China is changing! Pray for us!"

Ron MacMillan, Asia Correspondent for News Network International, has picked up this challenge. He writes: "wherever democracy has been established throughout the world, the Christian community has been instrumental in establishing it. Yet China is shaping up to be the historic exception. The sizable Christian community is not at the forefront of the "democracy fever" that has swept China's cities". MacMillan quotes a university student as saying: "as we studied the history of democracy, it became clear to us that democracy was not the *root* of freedom but a *fruit* of freedom. The more we looked, the more we realised that democracy's roots lie in Christianity. So now we are studying the Bible together, to see how we can bring democracy to China". But the poignancy of that comment, MacMillan argues, is that it is so unrepresentative of mainstream thought in the democracy movement.

Tony Lambert of OMF agrees. He calls for a model of evangelism amongst China's intellectuals that is thoroughly rooted in Scripture, calling for personal faith and repentance, and yet which does not flinch from grappling with social and political issues from a robust Christian viewpoint. This approach "sees political and social concern issuing naturally from a Biblical concern with the whole man. The Gospel is not political, but it

214

may issue in political concern. In a crisis such as this, Christians cannot be neutral in the face of monstrous injustice".

There is a challenge for us who are Christians. Do we, in Lambert's words, have anything "to offer groping Chinese intellectuals as they seek to rebuild their country on firm foundations"?

It is a challenge of enormous proportions and of historic significance. If, as Samuel Chadwick said, "prayer is the acid test of devotion", then let us pray for God to move on China as never before, to bring to many more the Way and the Truth and the Life. If, as we claim, we as Christians know the answer, let us see whether we will go East and pay a price for that great nation with our lives and our finances. The students gave their lives for what, in my opinion, they knew not clearly. We need to be willing to give as much for Him whom to know is eternal life.

CHAPTER 15

ISLANDS IN THE SHADOW

Having touched on the events that led up to and followed the massacre in the Tiananmen Square in May and June of 1989, I now need to make some reference to the two other communities of Chinese most directly effected by them — the Chinese in Hong Kong and in Taiwan. I do not intend to discuss Macao, a Portugese colony with a future parallel to Hong Kong's. The purpose of this chapter is not to look in depth at their situations. My terms of reference for this book are China, its church and the ministries relating to that nation and church. I intend to adhere to that narrow definition in this chapter. Of course that means that much will go unsaid regarding these two vital communities of Chinese — both of whom are affected in so many ways by China's past, present and future. Much is now being said about Hong Kong and the years leading up to 1997 in other publications. The same, to a slighter lesser extent, is true of Taiwan.

HONG KONG.

A number of months ago, Dennis Balcombe wrote some words that have now taken on a new and much more vital meaning. Dennis observed: "As far as Hong Kong is concerned, the whole future of this last British colony, (its) freedom of religion and the stability of the society, depends on what will happen in China during the next several years".

How prophetic those words are in the light of recent events. The Tiananmen events have completely destabilised Hong Kong. They have rocked its financial centres and stock market; they have increased from a flood to a torrent the numbers of people running to leave Hong Kong, and raised to thunder level the demands that the British government should allow another 3 million and more the right of access to Britain. For the first time the people of Hong Kong have joined in concerted, open and united political action. That and much more. Why? Because in 1997 those same PLA troops (the ones which gunned down and ran over innocent civilians) will be resident in Hong Kong's territory.

The menacing shadow of 1997 looms large over Hong Kong, for that is the date — but a few short years away — when the colony returns to Chinese rule. The agreement between the British and Chinese governments has already been signed. There is no turning back.

Hong Kong, with around 6 million people of predominantly Cantonese origin, is one of the most overcrowded places on the face of the earth. Refugees from Vietnam and illegal immigrants from China keep arriving in large numbers by boat and other means, only adding to the population problem. The Hong Kong Government has now closed its doors to the 'boat people' and other such immigrants. Once the refugees do arrive in Hong Kong, there is nowhere for them to go except into refugee camps, or to live in squalor on disused ferries. There just is no more room in the territory. For the greater majority of them, resettlement in other countries of the world remains highly unlikely, and their future is bleak. Some families have been in 'closed camps' for as long as seven years. The territory

— actually in the three different parts of Hong Kong, Kowloon and the New Territories — can no longer sustain them.

1997 is of vital importance to every aspect of the lives of the population of Hong Kong. That is obviously true of the financial sector. Hong Kong is one of the major financial markets in the world. A third of China's trade already passes through Hong Kong. It is also true of every other sector — political, industrial, social, cultural and religious. It is, however, only that last one, with particular reference to China, that I want to deal with in this section.

The first draft of the Basic Law that will apply to the Special Autonomous Region (SAR) of Hong Kong after 1997 was released on April 29th, 1988. In September of the same year it was made available to Hong Kong's citizens for five months of examination and response. The overriding concept of the Basic Law is of 'two systems, one country'. Most regard this, however, as practically unworkable. It is virtually impossible for Hong Kong to remain an independent power while under the sovereignty of China. The balance between the two concepts of local autonomy and national sovereignty is an unstable one. Such a policy could so easily change to 'one country, one system'. These fears are not allayed by the undue emphasis in the draft of the Basic Law on China's sovereignty, with insufficient measures to guarantee Hong Kong's autonomy.

Hong Kong citizens are entitled to ask their Northern neighbours a crucial question: "who is China?". Twice in recent years — at the end of the Cultural Revolution in 1976 and 13 years later with the "promotion" of Li Peng — we have seen violent and severe changes in ideological and humanitarian approaches within China. Historically, China is capable of more than a change of government. It is capable of a whole change of approach dictated by ideological fundamentals, an approach which can radically change its attitude to any and all internal and external laws. Most countries adhere to agreements — and the spirit of agreements — signed by previous administrations. In China that cannot be guaranteed. What one group may have in good faith agreed to before 1997 may not be seen as binding after 1997. If China's own legal system is still rudimentary and easily bypassed by her potentates, can the people of Hong Kong trust China to adhere to the Basic Law? Many think not.

In the complex web of facts and emotions surrounding the relevance of this to Christians and Christian ministries in Hong Kong, there are at least three points worthy of consideration:

1. The Basic Law's guarantees — or lack of them — to churches and Christians.

The clauses on religious freedom leave much to be desired. The document appears to guarantee that religious organisations will have a fairly high degree of independence. However, the sensitive issue of human rights needs more than a few general statements in the years that follow the Tiananmen massacre. Many feel that the document has omitted or insufficiently protected such key areas as the right to life, freedom from torture or degrading punishments, freedom of expression, freedom of movement and the right to a fair trial.

The signs are not good at the moment. Some familiar with the history of the TSPM in China itself warn that the same pattern may be used in Hong Kong. Some members of the Hong Kong Council of Churches have already stated that they are in favour of the TSPM. Many other Christians in Hong Kong have no desire whatsoever to be involved in any way with them. They do not see their own 'spokespersons' as representative.

A controversial article appeared in Hong Kong under the pen name of Xin Weisi, stressing that the church should not participate in any way in politics. The article was actually written by a group of writers from the New China News Agency, the Communist news agency in Hong Kong, but appeared to be from the pen of a Hong

Kong resident. Christians from Hong Kong are extremely anxious that such ideas do not get into the Basic Law.

2. The response from the Christians in Hong Kong. The voting with the feet syndrome.

How many of Hong Kong's citizens will actually remain to see the Communist takeover? Already there are clear signs of an increasing brain drain. Thousands of well-educated, middle management business and professional people are leaving the colony already. Over 45,000 did so in 1988. This will seriously affect the prosperity of the territory.

In the days and weeks following the Tiananmen massacres, the people of the colony have raised again as a major issue that of the rights of British passport holders (between three and three and a half million people in Hong Kong). As British law now stands, they do not have right of access to the UK. That means that they effectively cannot leave Hong Kong, unless they have the finance to buy themselves passports from other countries — and many do not. The issue was brought to a head by the reported failure of the British Embassy in Beijing to grant assistance to such passport holders (for example Hong Kong journalists) during the June 1989 troubles in Beijing. The issue of the future of these millions of people is an increasingly volatile one, which will not go away.

The business and commercial sector is not alone in being hurt by this problem of emigration. The church is also having to face this problem. The president of a Lutheran Theological Seminary has revealed that hundreds of young Hong Kong Christians are applying to seminaries in the United States. They are not alone. Many Christians, faced with all the possible ramifications of the Communist takeover, are wrestling as to whether to leave before the fateful day. The rich can emigrate to Britain, America, Canada or Australia, but the future looks decidedly less optimistic for those in the middle

221

and lower income group — who in fact make up the majority.

A significant number of church leaders are now considering a move to North America, leaving their churches to fend for themselves and face the future alone. Resentment is already beginning to surface about the number of pastors and leaders who had at one time stated that they would remain after 1997, but are quietly disappearing to the other side of the world for 'further study'. These same churches have, as yet, no coherent strategy laid out to train young leaders who can take over, whilst continuing to make their home in Hong Kong even after 1997.

The lay leadership of the church is largely made up of well educated, and financially comfortable businessmen and professional people. There is real concern that their continued exodus to the safety of other countries will cause a leadership crisis in the churches.

3. Attitudes to the China ministries based in Hong Kong.

Almost from the moment that Hong Kong became a British territory it became a base for intense Christian activity into the Mainland of China. When China's doors were closed to all outside influence, Hong Kong beamed gospel broadcasts from its radio stations to Chinese Christians hungry for the word of God. Bible and Christian literature ministries and much else have grown up over the years, all serving China's church. With 1997 drawing ever closer, the future of these China ministries based in the colony is a matter of serious concern.

On the secular side, the pattern is not encouraging. In the past year there have been a number of arrests and interrogations designed to discover information about organisations responsible for carrying Bibles into China. There is a concerted effort being made to narrow down the effective evangelical groups in Hong Kong, with a view to having them closed down before 1997. It is clear that Hong Kong people will not be allowed to witness

222

in any way into China.

The 'Three-mutual Policy' (non-interference, non-subordination and respect) in the Basic Law does place clear restrictions on Christians from Hong Kong conducting gospel ministry into the Mainland. It is possible that the Chinese authorities will try to remove the effective China ministries before 1997. Among these could be such key organisations as the Far Eastern Broadcasting Company, the Chinese Church Research Centre, Christian Communications Ltd and Asian Outreach. These are four of the main evangelical ministries working into China.

The attitude of the Protestant organisations within China to the China ministries based in Hong Kong is no more encouraging. In their official magazine, 'Tian Feng', the TSPM leadership recently launched a fierce attack on the China Ministries. It named such misdemeanours as 'secretly spreading the gospel, smuggling Bibles, and secretly setting up churches and theological seminaries'. The article was particularly unpleasant about Chinese nationals who had left China and were involved in the work of the Hong Kong based China ministries, denouncing them as traitors.

'Tian Feng' also denied the existence of any house church movement within China, stating that such a movement existed only in minds and imaginations of these Hong Kong groups. Claims that there were 50 million Christians worshipping in China were also denied. These claims were totally exaggerated — the number of Christians in China was hardly above 4 million. The inflated numbers, the article said, were used by China ministries to extract financial support from Christians around the world.

The article closed with a clear threat, quoting the Sino-British agreement. The TSPM interprets the relevant part of the agreement to mean that no person or organisation outside of China can be involved in evangelistic work of any kind on the Mainland without permission from the TSPM.

There was one further threat. If the article was not heeded, the TSPM/CCC would, in future, not invoke the principle of religious freedom to protect people acting in the ways described. This is interpreted to mean that the TSPM will put its weight behind the Chinese government in closing down all China ministries based in Hong Kong after 1997.

This attitude of the TSPM church leaders in China towards their Hong Kong brethren now hardly bodes well for the post-1997 period. Such all-out attacks on Hong Kong's evangelical ministries are hardly the run up to a mutually edifying cooperation in the cause of the Gospel. They show no sign of a desire for reconciliation and mutual honouring. How sad that such attacks are coming from the TSPM church leaders in China, rather than secular atheists! They involve classic character assassination of men of God.

These three factors point to a very unstable situation for the churches within Hong Kong and for the related China ministries. It is certainly not a time when those of us who live outside the colony need to point the finger. Which of us can say what we would do if we were living in Hong Kong in the years leading up to 1997?

There are no simple answers. It could even be, given the enormous tensions and conflicting interests, that there are no answers at all. What is clear is that the period leading up to 1997 is crucial, for Christians in Hong Kong and for Christians in China. It is equally clear that not many of us outside Hong Kong seem really troubled by that. That surely cannot be right.

I do not believe it is for me to suggest answers. That would be highly presumptuous. But I want to offer two suggestions, more concerned with spiritual attitude than political approaches.

Firstly, the period up to and beyond 1997 could be seen as a time of opportunity, where the gospel could be preached and received more widely than ever before in

Hong Kong. If China's lessons of blessing from pressure mean anything to Hong Kong, they must mean that a harvest of unprecedented proportions could be reaped in Hong Kong. It can be a time when the church commits itself to the colony unreservedly and plays its part in pushing back the tide of despair that is beginning to sweep over so many of its citizens. Hong Kong's materialism has drowned out the serious consideration of spiritual needs by her people. But this is a new and very different season, where the things of this world begin to look strangely dim in the light of the days to come. The churches have always had an answer; the problem was that noone was asking the question. Now they may well begin to.

Secondly, there is another lesson to learn from China. It concerns the power of prayer for nations and communities. We can change history through prayer and fasting, through a commitment to the kingdom of the Lord Jesus Christ. A major part of the answer lies not in Beijing, Hong Kong or London. It lies with the worldwide church of Jesus Christ, with the salt and light in that part of the world.

Perhaps those suggestions seem irrelevant and impractical. If they do, we might need to ask what agenda, as Christians, we have adopted. God's purpose is that men and women might be saved (2 Peter 3:9). He seems willing to allow much pressure upon nations and communities to permit us to be alerted to our need to come to saving faith in Jesus. I believe that is His present fundamental agenda for Hong Kong. I also believe that many of us should cooperate more fully with it.

★★★★★★★★★★★★★★★★★★★★★★

TAIWAN.

The situation looks uncertain and full of questions for Hong Kong. It does also for Taiwan. However, over the last few years three factors have come together to make

Taiwan a key place spiritually in China terms. I want to discuss them briefly. I have no desire to approach the matter from a political or economic standpoint, except as these matters affect the Gospel and the clear call from God to the church in Taiwan to reach out to China and its church.

i) Taiwan's reversal of attitude regarding contact with the Mainland of China.

I lived in Taiwan as a missionary from 1969-79. It was impossible to go to China then, because China was in the throws of the Cultural Revolution. I lived close to the ground in Taiwan — very deeply involved in student work with Campus Evangelical Fellowship, the island's equivalent to IVF/UCCF. I taught in Taiwan University and was advisor to the Christian Union there for several years. Some of the students I taught in university or in CU groups were destined for top US universities. I was involved in leadership of teams of students that went to the countryside to preach the Gospel. I preached very widely in churches in a large number of different denominations.

One thing that stood out during that time was the adamant position of the Taiwan government that they were at war with China. If they talked of going back to China, it was to 'liberate' the Mainland by military force.

At the end of 1987, Chiang Jingguo, son and heir of Chiang Kaishek, changed that. I personally feel that he knew he was near to death, and wanted to make his mark on history. Whatever the facts may be, his government opened the door cautiously to China, permitting Taiwan's citizens to return to China on visits if they had relatives there. I have pointed out earlier in the book that most of them do. The Taiwanese now are allowed to return to the Mainland for up to two months each year.

In early 1988, I asked a Taipei taxi-driver if he had been back to China yet. He was an older man whose accent told me that he had come from China in the late 40's. A few years before it would have brought a torrent of abuse about China, and threats of imminent invasion by the Taiwanese (ROC) army. But not now. No, he said, he was waiting till the summer, when the weather was warmer. Times had changed!

By January 1988, the month of that conversation, more than 31,000 Taiwanese had applied to visit the Chinese Mainland, taking advantage of the relaxation of the travel ban that had come into force only four months earlier. The numbers involved are indicative of the great desire in many people's hearts to return to their roots. The Taiwanese are quick to point out, however, that this relaxation of the travel ban in no way indicates a change in the political situation. They are still very definitely not open to talks on reunification.

Now there has been a cautious sporting exchange, open-armed welcomes by the Mainland of the returning Taiwanese, even a Taiwanese government official travelling to Beijing to attend a 'neutral' meeting of the World Bank. All of that would have been impossible a few years before. Taiwan still regards itself as at war with China. It holds its own government still to be the true government of China.

Taiwanese Christians have been praying for the day when they could go to China to evangelise, especially among their relatives who were left on the mainland. Now that day has come. This turn of events has created a marvellous opportunity. The Lord has opened up this door for Taiwanese Christians to reach into China with the gospel. The potential for this avenue of work is almost limitless. The Taiwanese have several advantages over Hong Kong Chinese. They speak Mandarin, the 'official' language of China, whereas most of the Hong Kong Chinese speak Cantonese. They have a deep love for their motherland, and because they are financially quite well off, they want and are able to support the work of the ministry into China.

We do not yet know what the long term reactions will be on the Taiwan side to the Tiananmen massacres and the Li Peng hardline posture. In the short term it has led to a yet wider door. The Taiwan government allowed direct mail and telephone communication to the Mainland for the first time since 1949. That was to try and break the media blackout that the Li Peng government had imposed — the version that says that no students died in the Square.

In the longer terms Taiwan's attitude and continued willingness to open its doors to China will depend on three factors. Firstly, how long Li Peng remains in power and Deng Xiaoping remains alive, imposing the current hardline policies. Secondly, whether the Taiwanese commitment to political confrontation or their equally strong commitment to economic flexibility prevails. Thirdly, what line their longtime allies, the USA, take — though that is probably a much less important factor than it was ten or twenty years ago.

I do not know the answer to those questions. I pray that the open door policy between the two will continue to grow more and more, for the sake of peace in the region and for the sake of the church in China. But I do know that as 1997 comes and goes, the Taiwanese will be watching very closely what happens in Hong Kong.

They have a difficult balancing act to endure. On the one hand, some of their own indigenous people are very strongly committed to the formation of the State of Taiwan, completely free from both the Republic of China and the People's Republic of China. On the other hand, China presses in on them to take back sovereignty of the 'province' of Taiwan.

It is yet another situation of deep complexity — and of deep opportunity for a praying and sending worldwide church.

ii) Taiwan's increasing prosperity and therefore economic potential for the Gospel.

There is no need for me to comment in depth about this. Most of us in the richer nations would find our wardrobes and electrical goods considerably depleted

were a thief suddenly to remove from us all that is
"MIT" — made in Taiwan. The island has proved
extremely flexible and able in riding the tides of
economic and industrial changes. They are, in certain
sectors, incredibly wealthy. The population of twenty
million have a US$75 billion foreign reserves strength —
at the moment more than West Germany! Taiwan is
America's third largest trading partner. It ranks
thirteenth in the world in industrial terms. Its gross
national product is two and a half times that of Hong
Kong and six times that of Singapore. The per capita
income of its people is US$6,000 a year. Evergreen, the
biggest container shipping company in the world, was
built and is owned by a Taiwanese. Taipei's cost of living
is twice that of Hong Kong *(The Independent, 26th June,
1989)*.

There is obviously a spill over there into the church.
They are not a poor church and they give generously,
not the least to the work of the Lord in Mainland China.
They see that as family giving to family, and they are
right to do so. They therefore represent a major and
committed source of finance to help the churches in
Mainland China.

iii) Taiwan's quickening in its spiritual atmosphere.

My own time in Taiwan was a hard one from the point
of view of seeing a deeper work of the Spirit there. Deep
prejudice prevailed amongst certain groups against the
charismatic work of the Spirit, on grounds that I can
very much sympathise with. One Chinese church in
South East Asia had so polluted these waters with its bad
and unloving testimony and its cavalier approach to the
word of God that it was easy for some to assume that
all charismatics must behave and believe like that.
Equally, some of the evangelical (and godly) missionary
societies took a hard and ungracious attitude to the
matter, much influencing the key Chinese churches and
para-church organisations.

There is, however the beginnings of a significant move of the Holy Spirit in Taiwan today. I would not call it more than that — a beginning. The signs are clear and encouraging. Some significant young leaders have been touched by God in new ways. Some young men in their 30's are seeing fast growing churches springing up. There is the sound of rustling in the trees!

Some of the effects of these three factors I have mentioned are already visible. One pastor from Taiwan decided to visit the village of his family in China. Once there he began to preach Christ. Before he had left he had baptised 120 new converts. At the baptism he told them that only those willing to suffer for Christ could be baptised, otherwise they should step back from the act of baptism. Practically all accepted baptism with this understanding that they were called to walk in the way of the cross.

Whilst the saying 'when one door closes, another opens' is certainly not Scriptural, it can often be true. God is sovereign over all the earth. The affairs of history, of nations and peoples are in His hand. Nothing takes Him by surprise. 1997 has not caught Him unawares. Even if that door to China via Hong Kong does comes under pressure, it would appear that another bridgehead is being built. There are thousands of Bible-believing Christians ready to go across that bridge, carrying the Gospel of truth with them. The Taiwanese will influence the nation of China in the way that China knows and understands best — through witnessing to family and to relatives. Whatever happens, God's will is to see His purposes fulfilled for the people of China on the Mainland and in Taiwan.

CHAPTER 16

CHOICES

China has seen great battles on epic scale over the years. Spiritually, the heart of the battle has been twofold. Firstly, to see the one true God honoured in the nation. Secondly, to find the men and women who will go forth in His Name to serve Him in the nation. Of course that is true in any nation, but we have seen it writ large in China. We have seen it in the 50's, as the party tried to kill the church by strangulation and injection of spiritual poison. We have seen it again in the Cultural Revolution, where they tried straight and immediate assassination. And yet the church flourishes, not dead, but living; not some withered tree, but a mighty tree under whose shade can rest an ever growing band of men and women.

God has always worked through men and women in China. Chinese church history shows that this emphasis has never changed. Littered with problems, crises, divisions and stands against heresies of one kind or another it may be, but there are precious names of men and of women that spring to mind when one considers the unfolding story of God's dealings with this great nation. Believers from inside and outside the nation,

231

whose lives burned like flaming torches in the darkness; who often stood against the tide of popular opinion; who risked everything, including their own lives, for the sake of their God and the people to whom they had been sent to serve.

What was it that made these people stand out in their generation? I believe it was simply that when God called, they responded. They were not disobedient to the vision for China and its church and its people that God placed in their hearts, but nurtured it, pursued it and saw it fulfilled, as far as they were able, in their lifetime.

In the missionary movement prior to 1949, dedication, sacrifice of comfort, health and even life are indicative of the calibre of the men and women who were prepared to obey the call of God, leave their homeland for a totally foreign culture and way of life, and seek to serve and win a people who were often aggressively hostile towards them. Protestant missions were motivated by a clear vision to preach the gospel where Christ had not been named. This vision was shared by those who stayed at home, many local churches and individuals contributing to the missionary effort through prayer and financial support. God looked for men and women who, knowing the dangers, would still be prepared to carry His word to the most heavily populated nation on earth, and He found them. Hundreds of people were prepared to leave the comfort of Western society to serve the Lord Jesus Christ and the people of China.

As He looks at China today, with one quarter of the world's population within its borders, does the Lord still find people willing to serve Him and the Chinese people at a time of possibly their greatest need? God is still looking for men and women to make an impact on China. The opportunities are there, the door is still open, but who knows how much time the church will be given to play its part? 60 percent of China's one billion people are under 35 years of age and many are open to the gospel. One in every three non-Christians on our planet is Chinese. That is the challenge of China, a challenge to which I believe every Christian must, at the very least, give serious and proper consideration.

A very great crowd of witnesses stands before us. Some few I have mentioned in this book. Morrison, Hudson Taylor, Watchman Nee, Wang Mingdao and others. Others — many, many others — have not been mentioned. Men and women of whom this world is not worthy — the John Sungs, the Gladys Aylwards and a countless host of others who loved the Lord and loved China. God found men and women to live and move and have their being for Him in China and for China.

CHOICES

If I were to search for a key to these men and women, amongst the many keys that come to mind, I would use one word — *choices*. Each one made certain choices, each choice in obedience to God or in disobedience. Out of right choices came the walk of obedience to God for His purposes in China. And out of the wrong choices came a walk that missed the purposes of God.

I remember talking to a missionary in Taiwan. He had been a missionary in China before 1949, and was now old and full of years. He shared with me how his father before him had been called to China, but he had never made it. After that call he had decided to delay obedience and make some money in oil speculation. It seemed an easy option, even if it ran contrary to God's leading in his life. He could be sure that it would not delay him long before he fell into step with God's plan for him in China. But he was wrong. He chose the wrong time and his company crashed. He spent most of the rest of his days trying to repay his creditors. He never made it to China.

Choices for China — or not for China.

★★★★★★★★★★★★★★★★★★★★★★

Please allow me to be personal. Not because I want in any way to compare myself with those names I have listed above. It is simply that I know my own story best. I know well that from one point of view my life — and yours — has been a series of choices.

I had to make a choice in York in 1967. As I have said, I had left Cambridge after 5 years of study there to work with David Watson in the exciting work that he was pastoring in the city. I was his first fulltime worker, and so much was new, fresh and exciting. Souls were being saved — many of them — and the church was growing fast.

But one night God spoke to me. I felt the presence of God so strongly that I went out late at night and walked the streets of York praying. I had been a year at York, and was enjoying my work. As I opened my heart to God, I felt him speak to me. "You are putting down roots here and I have not told you to do that." It had been natural to do so, because of the tremendous work of God that was taking place. But after God had spoken to me, I knew that I had to make specific moves to seeing His call on my life for China fulfilled. That meant choosing to leave York.

I wrote to Brother Andrew of Open Doors, whom I had got to know because of being involved in work in Eastern Europe. This was at the time of the Cultural Revolution in China, when there was absolutely no hope of getting into China to work. Brother Andrew wrote back to me with words of faith. "1969 is the year of opportunity," he said, and gave me the address of a doctor and his wife, Donald and Penny Dale, who were working in Taiwan. They were looking for someone to help with their clinic on the administration side while they were home on furlough. If someone could do that, they would guarantee that person's visa.

Literally with no income, and without the support of any missionary society, I felt God tell me to go to Taiwan. When I shared this with David Watson and the

234

people at St. Cuthberts, they very generously offered to support me. Every year, once a year, they would take up the Harvest Thanksgiving offering and give it to me. I had no idea how much this would be, but trusted God to take care of me.

God had spoken; I had to make a choice. Either to stay with David Watson in that thrilling environment in York, or take a step towards the Chinese people. To stay is the comfort zone of York and a comfortable and exciting church, or go to a land where I knew nobody, nor had a job lined up, nor had a secure income. I had made another choice.

Around 1975 I faced another choice. I was 31 years old, and unmarried. The choice then at that time was obvious! During my time at St. Cuthberts six years earlier I would occasionally meet 'secretly' in David's rectory with a young student called Christine Guillebaud to watch 'Hancock's Half Hour'. She was a first-year student at York University who came from a family of missionaries. Her parents had served in Africa, with the Ruanda Mission, in Rwanda, Uganda and Burundi; her grandparents had been missionaries also. Christine was clear from the beginning about our relationship, but I was not. One of the factors was my feeling that she was not called to China. But independently, in His sovereign mercy, God spoke to her through Brother Andrew in England while I was miles away in Taiwan.

The Lord was gracious there, because during the six years that I dithered she received marriage proposals from several different men, mostly clergymen, all of which were graciously and politely refused. Yet I believe, for all my dithering, God honoured the desire of my heart — that my life partner should know a common call to China. I may not have made the choice in the right way. But God honoured it, because it was made for China, by keeping for me a choice companion to love Jesus and China with me.

In 1984 came the choice that I have referred to

previously in the book — the one that took place on York Racecourse while I was waiting on God. "Take Derek Prince into China". Though at that time I did not know Derek, yet the result of that choice — that step of obedience — is one of the largest China ministries of any Western Bible teacher — radio programmes, books and tapes flooding into China, meeting the needs of that hungry church. It has not by any means been easy, with the pressure of the work to produce scripts, and the battles involved. But I do not regret for one second that I responded to that simple word on the racecourse. God gave me, in His sovereign mercy, the chance to touch millions of lives in China.

Towards the end of 1986 came another choice. As a result of much deliberation, Chinese Church Support Ministries (CCSM) was born. Since its official beginning in January 1987, it has grown considerably, with the workload increasing at such a rate that more full and part-time staff have had to be taken on to cope with the expansion of the ministry.

As the work of Chinese Church Support Ministries grew and flourished under God, I found myself facing yet another important choice in 1987. I had planted Acomb Christian Fellowship in York in the early 80's and pastored it from the beginning. For a number of years I had been the senior pastor among a group of fine leaders. Then God spoke to me again and told me that the next ten years of my life were to be dedicated to China. In response to this I sought the Lord for the future of the church and resigned as senior pastor, handing on to John Wilson, a capable and gifted brother.

I had made the choice between pastoring a local church in Acomb and giving more time to China. As it had always been throughout my life, right from the time that the nurse walked into my hospital room and asked me that unforgettable question about my future, China had to be the priority. The call of God was indelibly imprinted on my life and nothing could be allowed to deflect my vision from that high calling.

I cannot help feeling that those choices that Christine and I have made were so easy compared to those that so many have made for China. The 'loss' of 10 years of my life in Taiwan. The 'loss' of position as pastor and wife in a local church, and the "platform" that sometimes goes with that. The loss of time to build a wider ministry in the UK, because scripts or books or whatever for China demanded it. For Christine and the children, the 'loss' of a husband and father in journeyings often for China. Compared with what so many offered for China — including their lives — they are embarrassingly small choices.

Yet there is a vital point to draw from all of that. Out of those choices made have come ministry to China. Out of the obedience (if I may be so presumptuous as to call it that) of one couple have come those radio broadcasts and tapes and books for China; that challenging and working for prayer for China; that informing about practical needs in medical, educational and other fields for China; that encouraging and assisting of men and women to go as professionals to China; that raising of finance for CCSM to be able to work and for others to have resources for China.

Out of the slender obedience of one couple has come something concrete for China.

What would happen if it were not one couple, or one hundred couples, but the whole church who started making choices for China? What would happen if the whole church — your church together and you individually and as couples — started praying and giving and going to China? What would happen if we all took seriously the great commission of the One we call Lord and Master, Who said we were to go to the ends of the earth, even to China? If we took time off from our local, parochial concerns and lifted up our eyes to the harvest field of one billion people? What would happen if we made that choice together?

I do not know what would happen. But if one couple can reach a thousand, and CCSM and DPM through that one couple can reach tens of thousands, then surely an awakened church of Jesus Christ in the lands outside of China could reach millions and millions in China.

That is my heartcry for China.

POSTSCRIPT

The day after submitting this book to the printers I received a letter from Hong Kong. A godly colleague involved in China ministries, Curtis Jones, shared the following incident. Whether it is truth or fiction, it does sum up all that I have been trying to share.

A man in China was travelling up a narrow mountain path. In a moment of carelessness he slipped and fell off the ledge. In desperation, as he fell, he grabbed hold of some bushes and undergrowth. He hung there, separated from death only by his precarious grip, crying out for help to passers by. Some passed by but refused to respond. Eventually a young Christian came along the path. The man begged for his life: "Please help me ! I have been here for hours – I cannot hold on much longer!"

The Christian hesitated. He feared that if he tried to help he might fall to his death together with the man. As the Christian dithered in indecision, the man's cries grew more and more urgent. His strength was failing. Finally, the man's hands could hold on no longer. He fell far below to his death, crying out, "PLEASE CAN SOMEONE HELP ME".

It is said that the Christian later went mad – unable to forget the cry for help which he had ignored.

Such is the heartcry from China today.

CHINESE CHURCH SUPPORT MINISTRIES

"There are signs of a great work of God in China today."

In response to the needs of the Chinese Church and to the heartcry of its people, C.C.S.M. is working in these areas:-

PRAYER   Encouraging this vital ministry

RADIO   Working with Far Eastern Broadcasting Company and Derek Prince Ministries (DPM) to produce radio broadcasts five days a week into China

TAPES   Working with DPM to supply China's spiritually-hungry believers

LITERATURE   Producing tens of thousands of Christian books and booklets for China

MEDICAL   Assisting with various aid schemes

PROFESSIONALS Co-operating with others to send Christian teachers, doctors, engineers, etc. to China

FOR FURTHER INFORMATION: Please contact:

Ross Paterson, Director, Chinese Church Support Ministries, 2B Carr Lane, Acomb, York Y02 5HU United Kingdom

Telephone: York (0904) 781213   FAX: 0904 784603

FINANCIAL CONTRIBUTIONS may be sent to the above address (CCSM is a registered charity in the U.K. - No. 327709) or, for USA tax-deductible gifts, to CCSM, IOM, 2700 Todds Road, Lexington, KY. 40509, USA.

APPENDIX A

LIST OF AGENCIES

The following agencies provide information on China:-

Asian Outreach,
G.P.O. Box 3448, Hong Kong.

Chinese Church Research Centre,
P.O. Box 312, Shatin Central Post Office, New Territories, Hong Kong.

Chinese Church Support Ministries,
2B Carr Lane, Acomb, York Y02 5HU, United Kingdom.

Christian Communications Ltd.,
P.O. Box 95364, Tsimshatsui, Kowloon, Hong Kong.

Far Eastern Broadcasting Company,
P.O. Box 96789, Tsimshatsui Post Office, Kowloon, Hong Kong.

Institute of Chinese Studies and the Chinese World Mission Centre,
1605 E. Elizabeth Street, Pasadena, CA 91104 USA

Open Doors International Headquarters, PO Box 47, 3840 AA Harderwijk, Holland

Overseas Missionary Fellowship,
P.O. Box 70505, Kowloon Central Post Office, Hong Kong.

Revival Christian Church,
154 Prince Edward Road W., Kowloon, Hong Kong.

Trans World Radio,
545 Nathan Road, 10th Floor, Mong Kok, Hong Kong.

Youth with a Mission,
10 Borrett Road, Hong Kong.

APPENDIX B

RECOMMENDED READING

A number of sources have been used in the preparation of this book. In particular, I would like to acknowledge David Adeney's "China: The Church's Long March" for its comprehensive coverage. The following reading list includes titles recommended by David Adeney.

Adeney, David H.(1973), *China: Christian Students Face the Revolution*. Downers Grove, IL: Inter-Varsity Press.

Adeney, David H. (1985), *China: The Church's Long March*. Regal Books, USA: Overseas Missionary Fellowship.

Adeney, David H. (1978), *The Church in China Today and Lessons We Can Learn from It*. Christian Communications Ltd., Hong Kong.

Adeney, David H. (1978), *Men of Vision*. Living Books for All, Hong Kong.

Bonavia, David (1980), *The Chinese*. Lippincott and Crowell, New York.

Broomhall, A.J., *Hudson Taylor & China's Open Century (6 vols.)*. Hodder & Stoughton and Overseas Missionary Fellowship, England.

Brother David (1981), *God's Smuggler to China*. Hodder & Stoughton, London.

Brown, G. Thompson (1983), *Christianity in the People's Republic of China*. John Knox Press, Atlanta, USA.

Choy, L.F. (1981), *On Your Mark*. Christian Communications Ltd., Hong Kong.

Francis, Lesley (1985), *Winds of Change*. Overseas Missionary Fellowship, London.

Kauffman, P.E. (1981), *China the Emerging Challenge: A Christian Perspective*. Baker, Grand Rapids, USA.

Lawrence, Carl (1985), *The Church in China: How It Survives and Prospers under Communism*. Bethany House, Minneapolis.

Lyall, L.T., (1985), *God Reigns in China*. Hodder & Stoughton, London.

Lyall, L.T., (1985), *New Spring in China*. Zondervan, Grand Rapids, USA.

MacInnis, Donald E. (1972), *Religious Policy and Practice in Communist China*. Hodder & Stoughton, London.

Morrison, Peter (1984), *Making Friends with Mainland Chinese Students*. Christian Communications Ltd., Hong Kong.

Wallis, Arthur (1985). *China Miracle*. Kingsway Publications, England.

Wang Mingdao (1981), *A Stone Made Smooth*. Mayflower Christian Books, Southampton.